"Church takes time, patience, gentleness, ... hospitality, mutuality and peaceableness. In other words, church takes practice—this is the prophetic witness of the L'Arche communities not to the world, but to the church! And this prophetic witness is carried in this book by the gentle voice of Jean Vanier, the polemical one of Stanley Hauerwas, and the wise introduction and conclusion from John Swinton. Here is the prophetic edge that is even at the vanguard of the emerging church!"

Amos Yong, professor of theology and mission, Fuller Theological Seminary

"Like the L'Arche communities, this book calls us to a humanism that is tender, patient and present. Its humanism is rooted in the incarnation, for 'the Word became flesh to bring people together' (Vanier), and is lived in the church, which proclaims a 'politics of gentleness' (Hauerwas)."

The Christian Century

"Theologian Stanley Hauerwas and L'Arche founder Jean Vanier discuss how these caring communities for persons with disabilities can teach the church about peace and acceptance. Full of personal experiences, this easy read makes profound observations about acceptance of suffering and disability, the important of relationship over power, and the slow daily work of creating peace in everyday life."

Mennonite Brethren Herald

"The questions raised and the reflections offered on those questions are indispensable for anyone living with, working with, or reflecting on those with mental disabilities."

Ethics & Medicine

STANLEY HAUERWAS
and JEAN VANIER

LIVING

GENTLY

in a

VIOLENT

WORLD

THE PROPHETIC WITNESS
OF WEAKNESS

EXPANDED EDITION

An imprint of InterVarsity Press
Downers Grove, Illinois

InterVarsity Press
P.O. Box 1400, Downers Grove, IL 60515-1426
ivpress.com
email@ivpress.com

Second edition ©2018 by Stanley Hauerwas and Jean Vanier
First edition ©2008 by Stanley Hauerwas and Jean Vanier

InterVarsity Press® is the book-publishing division of InterVarsity Christian Fellowship/USA®, a movement of students and faculty active on campus at hundreds of universities, colleges, and schools of nursing in the United States of America, and a member movement of the International Fellowship of Evangelical Students. For information about local and regional activities, visit intervarsity.org.

All Scripture quotations, unless otherwise indicated, are taken from the New American Standard Bible®, copyright 1960, 1962, 1963, 1968, 1971, 1972, 1973, 1975, 1977, 1995 by The Lockman Foundation. Used by permission.

While any stories in this book are true, some names and identifying information may have been changed to protect the privacy of individuals.

Cover design: David Fassett
Images: © Seb Oliver /Getty Images

ISBN 978-0-8308-3496-9 (print)
ISBN 978-0-8308-7391-3 (digital)

Printed in the United States of America ∞

InterVarsity Press is committed to ecological stewardship and to the conservation of natural resources in all our operations. This book was printed using sustainably sourced paper.

Library of Congress Cataloging-in-Publication Data

A catalog record for this book is available from the Library of Congress.

P 27 26 25 24 23 22 21 20 19 18 17 16 15 14 13 12 11 10 9 8 7 6 5 4 3 2 1

Y 41 40 39 38 37 36 35 34 33 32 31 30 29 28 27 26 25 24 23 22 21 20 19 18

Contents

Introduction

Living Gently in a Violent World

JOHN SWINTON

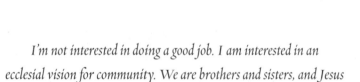

*I'm not interested in doing a good job. I am interested in an
ecclesial vision for community. We are brothers and sisters, and Jesus
is calling us from the pyramid to become a body.*

Jean Vanier

Before I entered academia I spent many years as a psychiatric nurse and then as a mental health chaplain working alongside people with various forms of mental illness and intellectual disability. Unlike many of my mental health colleagues, I was never very interested in the diagnosis or etiology of people's conditions. Even though I was young, I recognized that diagnoses and labels do not accurately represent people. In fact, these explanations can lead to destructive labels and stigmatizing assumptions that devastate their recipients. What did interest me was how people with these life experiences viewed the world. They saw things differently. And when I listened carefully, those whom the world called "mad" or "disabled" became a conduit that allowed me—and anyone else who chose to look and listen—to receive a different truth in the midst of a world that loves to deceive.

In chapter three of this book Jean Vanier tells us, "I realize as I get older that I have difficulty meeting so-called normal people. I don't know what to talk about. I can fool around at the dinner table with people with disabilities, but I can see that I am becoming marginalized. I know it is important to speak to the wider world. But it is not always easy when you discover you are living in two worlds." I know what he means. Negotiating the world of disability and the world of people who don't consider themselves disabled can be tragic, frustrating and deeply joyful all at the same time! But such encounters carry the potential to transform our friendships, our politics and our spirituality.

Marginalization is often the primary currency used by the citizens of both worlds.[1] But the dialogue between these two worlds is vital for the church to be the church and for the world to recognize Jesus and be transformed. Taking seriously the "world of the disabled" and allowing our perspectives to be shaped and changed by listening carefully to those who see things differently is a prophetic ministry of transformation and hope that all of us need to engage in if we are to live faithfully. One of the hopes of the authors of this book is that the essays presented here will help you the reader to become "odd," to see the world differently and thereby recognize the prophetic nature of that oddness for faithful discipleship. So a warning: By the time you've finished reading, your friends may start to think you're a little strange!

SEEING THE WORLD DIFFERENTLY

The society we in the West inhabit is a strange place. We are oddly comfortable with truths that, on reflection, are deeply dissonant and even disturbing. For example, we seem quite comfortable with the knowledge that up to twenty thousand children die every day from preventable diseases. We miss the deep irony that we constantly seek peace by going to war. We develop policies and practices that welcome people with disabilities into our communities, offering them rights and responsibilities, and at precisely the same time we develop forms of genetic technology designed to prevent them from entering society in the first place.

If Vanier is correct that in France within the next few years there will be no children born with Down syndrome because they will all have been aborted, then something is deeply wrong with our society. As my friend John, who has Down syndrome, puts it, "That doesn't make us feel very welcome, does it?"[2] And he's right. Stanley Hauerwas correctly points out in chapter two that one of the real dangers for people with disabilities in Western cultures is compassion! Our desire to alleviate perceived suffering in the name of compassion easily leads to the destruction of people whom God has created and loves beyond all things. How odd. I suspect that the question of precisely whose "suffering" we are alleviating in aborting children with disabilities will depend on whom we ask. It is rare for our society to take the time to ask people with disabilities. How odd.

Signing in heaven? Over the past few years those of us involved in practical theology at the University of Aberdeen have worked alongside people with disabilities in various forms of participatory research. This research is designed to help us work through key issues relating to disability, theology, church and society, and to explore the meaning of lives lived well with disability.[3] Part of our work has involved listening carefully to the stories of people with disabilities. As we have been drawn into the "strange world of disability" and learned how to hear the transforming narratives people have shared with us, our understandings, perspectives, values and expectations have changed. As we approach the work of Vanier and Hauerwas in this book, it will reward us to listen to two such prophetic voices. Let's begin with Angela.

A couple of years ago I was teaching a course on pastoral care. It was a distance-learning course, which meant that some people were in a classroom in Aberdeen and others were on the telephone throughout the United Kingdom. On that occasion the class was made up of people with differing backgrounds and perspectives. Among these was one person who had no sight and another who was profoundly deaf and spoke through an interpreter. At one point in the class, people were sharing their various spiritual experiences. The woman who was deaf, Angela, began to tell us about a dream she'd had. In that dream she had met with Jesus in heaven. She and Jesus talked for some time, and she said she had never experienced such peace and joy. "Jesus was everything I had hoped he would be," she said. *"And his signing was amazing!"*

For Angela, heaven's perfection did not involve being "healed" of her deafness. Rather, it was a place where the social, relational and communication barriers that restricted her life in the present no longer existed. What had been a "disability" now became the norm; that which had led to exclusion, anxiety, separation and loss of opportunity now became the precise mode in which Jesus addressed her. As we listen to Angela's story our minds are renewed (Romans 12:2) and we are freed to see Jesus differently as he speaks to us from his residence within the "strange world" of disability. How odd.

Renarrating the world. Dianne, a young woman with Down syndrome, also challenges us to see the world differently. When asked to describe how she experiences her spirituality, Dianne says, "I was born with a hole in my heart. When I was little it needed a patch and I was very ill.

It might be because of this but I have always felt special. . . . God is my best friend. God made me special because I was special to him."[4]

What is perhaps most startling about Dianne's description of her relationship with God is the way she turns the cultural narrative of disability on its head, countering many prevalent ideas about suffering and compassion. For example, a traditional theological discussion of someone in her situation often focuses on theodicy: "How can a good and loving God allow such deformity and suffering?" On the other hand, our liberal cultural assumptions often insist, "Isn't it better and more compassionate not to allow such people to exist at all?" Dianne does not allow such positions to masquerade as orthodoxy; she renarrates cultural and theological myths, and reframes her disability in the light of the truth that God loves her just as she is.

Rather than raising questions about whether God is good and loving, Dianne's disability draws her into the very presence of God and marks her out as special. Society often uses the term *special* in negative ways ("special needs," "special education"), but Dianne places it in the frame of love. To recognize one's own specialness is a gateway to friendship with God. It makes a radical political statement in a world that often forgets who we are and traps us in complex webs of labels, stereotypes, caricatures and false assumptions. In her gentle description of divine recognition, Dianne reveals a politics that stands in stark contrast to the politics of the world——a mode of politics that, as we shall see in chapter four, is the very essence of the coming kingdom of God.

Dianne's and Angela's stories draw together some of the key elements of this book. In uncovering the oddness of many of our cultural and theological assumptions about disability, they resonate deeply with the thinking of Hauerwas and Vanier presented in the essays to come. Both authors have noticed the types of cultural dissonance that Dianne highlights, and both (in different ways) offer us new modes of framing and entering the strange world of disability. Indeed, as we listen to the voices of Angela, Dianne, Stanley Hauerwas and Jean Vanier, it becomes clear that it is not the world of disability that is strange, but the world "outside," which we dare to call normal. It turns out that the world of disability is the place God chooses to inhabit.

How This Book Came to Be

The essays presented in this book emerged from a unique conference organized by the Centre for Spirituality, Health and Disability at the University of Aberdeen (www.abdn.ac.uk/cshad). In 2006 we invited Hauerwas and Vanier to come to Scotland to spend two days together, discussing and reflecting on important issues of disability and theology. They had not met before, though Hauerwas had written many times on the importance of Vanier's work and the significance of the L'Arche communities. Perhaps one of the most important aspects of the event was that these two men graced one another with the gift of friendship, a friendship that I suspect will last into eternity.

Hauerwas and Vanier spent two fascinating days sharing both publicly and privately their thoughts, joys and concerns surrounding the issue of disability and, in particular, around the question, "What does L'Arche have to say to the church?" All of us sensed that the church is in crisis, that there is a need for a shift from lukewarmness to faithfulness, from alienation to friendship with God and one another. Indeed, addressing this need is critical if the church truly desires to live its mission to the world and to honor the God who is love. Their gentle conversations began to tease out the implications of the church's situation and to start to think through what disability can tell all of us about the nature of God and of faithful discipleship.

Both Vanier and Hauerwas note that honoring such a God requires us to recognize the fundamental gospel principle that the weakest and least presentable people are indispensable to the church (1 Corinthians 12:22). However, to quote Vanier's words in chapter three, "I have never seen this as the first line of a book on ecclesiology! Who believes it?" Vanier and Hauerwas believe it. This book is an attempt to help us begin also to do so.

WHY L'ARCHE?

A vital aspect of a paradigm shift is the need for exemplars—

people or groups who can model the new paradigm, challenge our presuppositions and draw us into the belief that the new paradigm might actually be possible.[5] L'Arche is precisely such an exemplar. Jean Vanier founded the L'Arche communities in 1964, initially by simply living with two people with profound intellectual disabilities. Since then the L'Arche communities, with their fundamental ethos of "living with" rather than "doing for," have become an international network of communities in which people with intellectual disabilities live with people who do not share that life experience. They do not live together as carer and cared for but as fellow human beings who share care and need. The L'Arche communities provide a unique model of inclusiveness underpinned by a profound Catholic spirituality and theology. L'Arche is truly odd—it refuses to do what society thinks it should.

L'Arche as a sign and sacrament. This refusal to conform to societal norms has caused Hauerwas to see L'Arche as a powerful exemplar of the community God gave us as a marker for our redemption: the church. He views the L'Arche communities as witnesses to the reality that the Christian story is both true and livable. For Hauerwas, "Christianity is unintelligible without witnesses, that is, without people whose practices exhibit their committed assent to a particular way of structuring the whole."[6] Christianity is much more than an idea, he says: "Rather it is a bodily faith that must be seen to be believed."[7]

L'Arche shows, as the church is called to show, that Christianity is true by demonstrating what community would look like if the gospel were true. Unlike learning moral principles, following Jesus requires a change of heart. "The very content of Christian connections requires the self to be transformed if we are adequately to see the truth of [its] convictions."[8] L'Arche is a sign of hope and new possibilities, but above all it is a marker for the truth of the gospel; it is living proof that the story Christians bear is not fantasy or a collection of abstract principles but real and true and revealed clearly. When we view L'Arche this way, we begin to see how the question "What does L'Arche mean for the church?" might have implications far beyond the idea that disability theology is a "specialist interest." It is the heart of the gospel.

Unlikely allies? At first sight Jean Vanier and Stanley Hauerwas seem unlikely allies. Hauerwas (named America's best theologian by *Time* magazine in 2001) is a battle-hardened academic whose natural inclination is to defend people with intellectual disabilities by using his well-honed intellectual skills. As he says in chapter four, he sees himself as "a warrior on behalf of L'Arche, doing battle against the politics that threaten to destroy these gentle communities." At one level he stands in stark contrast to the gentleness of Jean Vanier and L'Arche. He states, "Where I see an enemy to be defeated, he [Vanier] sees a wound that needs to be healed. That's a deep difference."

And yet Vanier is no less of a warrior. He has fought many a hard battle as L'Arche has taken shape.[9] He is gentle, but, as we shall see, he also has the capacity for violence because, like all of us, he carries the deep wound of his own loneliness. But unlike many of us, he has learned to see his enemies as wounded people who are loved by God. Though it did not come easily or naturally, he learned gentleness as he allowed his experiences with people with profound disabilities to shape his presumptions and behaviors.

Gentleness is a vital dimension of the kingdom of God (Matthew 11:28-30), but it is a learned skill that requires work and demands patience, slowness and timefulness.[10] Such work means that we have to become "friends of time," a patient people who recognize that "we have all the time we need to do what needs to be done." Such friends of time seek to develop the patience to slow down, to recognize that our lives are not our own creation and that the God who filled the universe with beauty and who created all of us (Psalm 22:9-10) always finds time to be with us, to sit with us and to move us to a place in history we can call our own.

In recognizing the gift of creation and of our lives, we are freed to live differently. Like Dianne and Angela, we are freed to renarrate our lives in light of Jesus' revelation and the hopeful presence of L'Arche. In other words, we are freed to love. We are freed to greet one another with a holy kiss (Romans 16:16) and, as Josef Pieper puts it, to offer one another the words of love: "It's good that you exist; it's good that you are in this world."[11] The essays in this book offer a beginning place for all of us to start to do this. We offer them to you as transformative gifts. We pray that they may bring you many blessings.

1

The Fragility of L'Arche
and the Friendship of God

JEAN VANIER

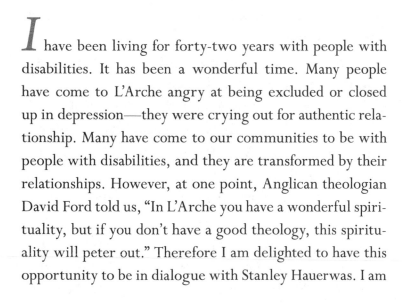

I have been living for forty-two years with people with disabilities. It has been a wonderful time. Many people have come to L'Arche angry at being excluded or closed up in depression—they were crying out for authentic relationship. Many have come to our communities to be with people with disabilities, and they are transformed by their relationships. However, at one point, Anglican theologian David Ford told us, "In L'Arche you have a wonderful spirituality, but if you don't have a good theology, this spirituality will peter out." Therefore I am delighted to have this opportunity to be in dialogue with Stanley Hauerwas. I am sure this will help me and many in L'Arche to strengthen the foundation of our theology.

I want to begin by saying something about knowing and not knowing. I love chapter two of the Gospel of John when Jesus brings the disciples to a wedding feast. It is a wonderful moment of celebration and relaxation, showing us that our life is to be enjoyed and that we are all called to a feast. At the wedding feast of unity, people drink lots and laugh and have fun. It is a time of togetherness and friendliness. And I imagine that Jesus came to this feast to have fun. I don't think he looked at his watch (which he didn't have) and said, "I must hurry and do a miracle there because they need me!" No, Jesus at Cana was having fun. Mary saw that the wine was running out, knew that the family would be humiliated, and asked Jesus to do something about it. There's something profoundly human about Jesus—the first thing he does in John's Gospel is to turn water into wine so a bride's father won't be embarrassed.

Later on in John 3, something else happens that I've always loved. A leader of the Jews named Nicodemus comes to see Jesus and says, "We know that a guy like you, with all the stuff you are doing, must be sent by God." Jesus replies in his enigmatic way that we must all be born from on high; he continues to say that we shouldn't be surprised to learn this because we can hear the wind—maybe even feel it on our faces—but we don't know where it's coming from or where it's going. So it is with things of the Spirit. You don't quite know where you are coming from or where you are going. And so it is with L'Arche. We don't quite know where we are going.

My life has been privileged enough that I never knew quite where I was going. I knew a little about where I was coming from, but I wasn't quite sure where I was going to. I left my home in Canada in 1942, at the age of thirteen, to join the British Navy. God knows why my father said I could do it. I joined knowing nothing, and I left the Navy in 1950, not knowing why I'd left except that I had been propelled into the gospel. That's when I met Father Thomas Philippe, who had founded a community in France for young people searching for their way in life. Father Thomas was a man of God. But I still had no idea where I was going.

Years went by and things fell into place. In 1963 Father Thomas had become chaplain of a small institution for people with disabilities. Because I wanted to be close to this priest, I discovered the terrible ways people with disabilities were treated. Why not do something for them? But what to do? God knows I didn't know. I wasn't a social worker. Having finished a Ph.D. in philosophy, I knew quite a bit about Aristotle, but beyond that, my knowledge was pretty limited!

I was able to buy a small house in the village where Father Thomas lived, and I met two men with severe disabilities who had been locked up in a dismal institution. We started living together. I was naïve—I thought I was going to do a little bit of good to Raphael and Philippe. But things started happening. People arrived to assist me, and six months later I was asked to take over the establishment where Father Thomas was chaplain. We moved from a very prophetic, small community to an institution for thirty people with disabilities. I knew nothing about how to run an institution.

Five years later I was asked to go to India, so I went to India. Within a year, a L'Arche community began in Bangalore with Hindus and Muslims. I knew nothing about inter-religious cooperation. Later a community started in the United Kingdom, which, of course, was ecumenical. But all I knew was the Roman Catholic Church. For me, to be ecumenical meant having a priest come to perform mass every day and getting permission for all the Anglicans to participate with the Roman Catholics. We only discovered little by little what it really meant to be ecumenical.

Today the challenges we face in L'Arche are very different. Governments give orders about how large bedrooms, bathrooms and corridors should be. Of the twenty-eight little houses in the areas where L'Arche started, eighteen have had to be remodeled. In my own particular community, about sixty people with disabilities live in nine homes, and sixty others live with their families and come to work in our workshops. About a hundred assistants are present in this community, and nearly half are volunteers. But the government passed a law recently, making it difficult for volunteers to come to L'Arche. We had to struggle with the legislators tremendously—if we had no volunteers, our communities would be in severe difficulty and many young people would not benefit from the friendships of our members with disabilities.

Things eventually worked out, but L'Arche is a fragile reality. Will it still be here in twenty years? There will always be people with disabilities, but will there always be people who want to live with them as brothers and sisters in community, in a place of belonging that helps each member, each person, grow to greater freedom? L'Arche is also a complex and beautiful reality—a place of transformation. People arrive and people leave—even the people with disabilities leave. Some get married. Looking back on the story of L'Arche, we can see how many people have been transformed.

I think of Janine, who came to L'Arche at the age of forty with one arm and one leg paralyzed. She experienced epileptic seizures and had difficulties understanding and learning. There was a huge amount of anger in her. She didn't want to come to L'Arche; she wanted to stay with her sisters, but she was terribly jealous of them because they had many children and she couldn't have any. To be placed in L'Arche was the last thing she wanted. She needed to express her anger, so she broke things and screamed and yelled. We took a lot of time to reflect, to try to understand where the anger was coming from. She was angry with her body, angry with her sisters, angry with God, angry because she didn't want to work in our workshops. But gradually, gradually, she discovered who she was and that she was listened to, understood and loved.

Janine used to love those old French Parisian songs that most people don't remember now. She loved singing them, and she discovered that she could dance to those songs and that other people appreciated them as well. Then she discovered something extraordinary: she was loved by God. She asked to be baptized and learned that we needed her to pray for us and our broken world. The last three years of her life were beautiful. I used to go and sit down beside her sometimes; she would see that I was tired and would put her hand on my head, saying, "Poor old man."

It is not easy to name how and when Janine's transformation took place, but somehow it did, as it has for many at L'Arche. Transformation has to do with the way the walls separating us from others and from our deepest self begin to disappear. Between all of us fragile human beings stand walls built on loneliness and the absence of God, walls built on fear—fear that becomes depression or a compulsion to prove that we are special.

Many assistants who come to us are also transformed. One young woman came to L'Arche at the age of seventeen like a wounded sparrow. Her parents had divorced. She was fed up with school, which forced her to learn things she did not want to learn. She had heard about L'Arche from her aunt. She came, and she was healed by people with disabilities who loved her and trusted her. So she began to trust and love herself. She became responsible for a home with ten severely disabled people. She left us after five years as a mature woman, going to Peru to work with kids in the streets.

What makes such transformation possible? Jesus says that when we're born of the Spirit, we don't know where that Spirit is coming from or where it's going—there is a reason for not knowing. Transformation gives us the audacity to advance along a road of unknowing. At the same time we can't be totally unknowing. There must be points of reference, particularly today as we participate in complex interreligious dialogue. We face, for example, the desire of a group of people in Kuwait to create a new community in their country. The group is led by a Muslim woman who spent some time in our L'Arche community in Syria. With our help, this group has spent three years reflecting on the conditions necessary for a L'Arche community to begin in Kuwait. To be a L'Arche community it will be necessary for them to affirm, "We are a Muslim group that also welcomes people from other religions." Just as in my community in France we welcome a number of Muslims, so the desire of this Kuwaiti group is to be interreligious. In L'Arche we have always had to work at interreligious cooperation, and today we are confronted with many new realities.

There is always uncertainty about how L'Arche will go on. But we have learned over the years to nurture the belief that God is protecting us. As I read Kathryn Spink's book on L'Arche, *The Miracle, the Story, and the Message*, I see how often we were not understood and sometimes rejected. Authorities in Rome, for example, didn't want to work with us because we were not exclusively Roman Catholic. They asked me, "Are you Catholic?" I said, "Yes, I am, but not all the members of L'Arche are. Catholics and Protestants, Hindus and Muslims, people with disabilities and assistants—they are all our brothers and sisters." The authorities broke off dialogue with us at this point, though with time the relationship was reestablished.

So life has not always been easy. But we've kept going. There is a vital need to listen to each other, to pray together, to listen to reality, to listen to God. We are at a point in our history where many of the people who come to serve and live in communities hardly know why they are there. Many do not have much Christian faith. So you see that there are many complexities in L'Arche. "Good" religious people don't always come to us; we get the ones who don't quite know what it means to be a "good" religious person and who will discover simply that to be a Christian is to grow in compassion.

MINDING THE GAP

In L'Arche we are searching our way. We are trying to understand. We do not have all the answers. But the vital thing is to remember and to tell the story of how it all began. And the story begins with a huge gap of injustice and pain. It is the gap between the so-called "normal" world and the people who have been pushed aside, put into institutions, excluded from our societies because they are weak and vulnerable or even killed before birth. This gap is a place of invitation in which we call people to respond.

We have to come back to the gospel vision. When I reflect on the gospel vision, I find that it is incredible. It is a promise that we human beings can get together. It is a vision of unity, peace and acceptance. It is a promise that the walls between people and between groups can fall, but this will not be accomplished by force. It will come about through a change of heart—through transformation. It will begin at the bottom of the ladder of our societies. Jesus didn't spend too much time in the rich cities of Israel, such as Tiberias. He spent time with people who were caught in prostitution, the people they called "sinners" who were excluded from the temple. He spent time creating relationships. That's what Jesus did. His vision was to bring together all the children of God dispersed throughout the world. God cannot stand walls of fear and division. The vision of Jesus shows us that division is healed by dialogue and by meeting together.

In the parable of the Good Samaritan, Jesus tells us that the Samaritan knew what to do. He picked up the injured Jew from the side of the road and took care of him. He put him on his own donkey, carried him to an inn and spent the evening with him. They talked, and they realized they were brothers in humanity. These two men met and spent time together. And both were transformed. Their prejudices fell away.

Throughout the Gospels there is a contrast between those who are well-integrated in society but are too busy and those who are excluded from society and have too much time. In the parable of the wedding feast (Matthew 22; Luke 14), some people are too caught up in short-term projects—marrying off a daughter or buying land. They have no time for the banquet of love. So the king, or the head of the house, tells the servants to go out into the highways and byways and bring in all the excluded—the poor, the people with disabilities, the blind. Bring them all in. And they come running to the banquet of love.

Paul says in 1 Corinthians 1 that God has chosen the weak, the foolish and the crazy to shame the clever and the powerful; he has chosen the most despised, the people right at the bottom of society. Through this teaching we see a vision unfold in which a pyramid of hierarchy is changed into a body, beginning at the bottom. One might ask if that means Jesus loves the weak more than the strong. No; that is not it. The mystery of people with disabilities is that they long for authentic and loving relationships more than for power. They are not obsessed with being well-situated in a group that offers acclaim and promotion. They are crying for what matters most: love. And God hears their cry because in some way they respond to the cry of God, which is to give love.

That was my experience the first time I entered an institution. The cry of people with disabilities was a very simple cry: Do you love me? That's what they were asking. And that awoke something deep within me because that was also my fundamental cry. I knew I could be a success. I had done well in the Navy. I had a doctorate in philosophy. I knew I could go up the ladder, but I didn't know whether I was really loved. If I fell sick, who would be there? I knew the need for admiration. I knew the need to be both accepted and admired. But something deep down within me didn't know if anybody really loved and cared for me as a person, not just for my accomplishments.

I had left my parents when I was thirteen. I knew they loved me, but I didn't feel in any way called to stay with my family. Something was awakened within me as I started to visit people with disabilities and heard their primal cry for relationship; it became clear to me that Jesus was at ease with people yearning for love. I began to understand that these people could help me grow in the wisdom of love. They would help me grow in a relationship with Jesus. It did not matter if people thought I was crazy.

We had lots of questions when we began communities in India. Interreligious dialogue or living together is never easy. We sought our own way. We had a little chapel and we put a tiny cross at the center. Then Mohanraj came to us, bringing with him a big picture of Ganesh. Ganesh is a Hindu god in the form of an elephant. We Christians are more used to doves than elephants. But elephants are strong and can remove obstacles and blockages. What were we to do with Mohanraj and his picture of Ganesh? Mohanraj had always prayed in front of this image. But we could already hear all the things some Christians might say if they visited. We didn't know what to do. It took time to find the right balance. Eventually Mohanraj's family took him back. We no longer kept the picture of the god Ganesh.

There are many things about people with intellectual disabilities that I do not understand, and I don't know how to communicate well with each one. But gradually, over the years, I have learned many things from them and about them—primarily, that within these people is an openness to God. And their longing for closeness with God is felt on a personal, intimate level. I don't know whether it's just the culture of my community in France, but I never hear a person with a disability talking about "Christ" or "the Lord." They only talk about "Jesus," using his little name. We also talk about Mary, his mother, and I'm always moved by the intimacy with which those names are spoken in our community. People with disabilities realize there is holiness there.

Over the last forty-two years we've had many deaths, and we've spent a lot of time celebrating death. It's very fundamental to our community. To celebrate death is to gather around and talk about the person—about Janine, for example, who died recently. We gathered to say how beautiful she was, how much she had brought to us. Her sisters came, and we wept and laughed at the same time. We wept because she was gone, but we laughed because she did so many beautiful things.

I remember when Francois, an assistant, died. Jean Louis, who walks with a walker, and Philippe, who has cerebral palsy, came and approached the place where Francois's body lay. They said to Jacqueline, "Can we say hello to Francois?" She said, "Of course," and they went up and looked at Francois. Then they said, "Can we kiss him?" She said, "Sure." They bent over reverently. "Oh sh—t, he's cold!" one of them exclaimed. As they hobbled out, one said to the other, "Mummy will be so surprised when she knows I kissed a dead person."

We begin to open up and accept our own handicaps when we accept death. Kissing and touching somebody who is dead has to do with accepting our own death, and that's why it's vital that we celebrate it. Jean Louis and Philippe taught me about accepting death.

The simplicity of our people, their closeness to God, helps us understand also that there should be no ideology of receiving holy Communion at the Eucharist. Sometimes we hear from parents, "I want my child to go to Communion." But does the child want to go? That is the question. We should never have an ideology of mandatory Communion but be open to desire. Communion in our communities is not just receiving consecrated bread; it is the satisfaction of a deep yearning for communion in the hearts of people with disabilities. They are called to become saints, people of communion with others.

LEARNING TO SEE THE HOLY

There are many holy people in our communities, but it is not always easy for people to see this if they do not share the conviction that the meaning of life is to become holy and prayerful. Every time I leave the community, Pascal comes up to me and gestures to say, "I will be praying for you." I believe in his prayer. I believe we can ask people with disabilities to help us.

Jacqueline, who began L'Arche with me many years ago, now has Parkinson's disease. We couldn't keep her in the community, so she is in an assisted-living facility. I see her as often as I can. But what really brings her alive is when I say, "I need you to offer what you're living as a prayer for us." As we get weaker and poorer, the challenge is to believe that the cry of the poor truly is a cry to God. God listens to the cry of the poor.

Does the church really believe in the holiness of people with disabilities? Some people believe the church should do good things for the poor. But do we believe in their holiness? I get upset when people tell me, "You're doing a good job." I'm not interested in doing a good job. I am interested in an ecclesial vision for community and in living in a gospel-based community with people with disabilities. We are brothers and sisters together, and Jesus is calling us from a pyramidal society to become a body.

A fundamental text for L'Arche is Luke 14:12-14, where Jesus says, "When you give a meal, don't invite the members of your clan, members of your family, your brothers, your sisters, your rich neighbors and your friends. Don't invite those that you normally get together with to flatter each other." This is what people usually do when they throw a party. They invite their clan. One person says, "You're super." The other says, "No, you're super! You gave me good wine last time. I will give you good wine next time." This is Aristotle's vision of friendship—sharing among equals. But Jesus says, "No, when you give a banquet—a really good meal—invite the poor, the lame, the disabled and the blind. Invite those who are excluded, and you shall be blessed." You will be repaid in the kingdom's currency. If you become a friend of somebody who is excluded, you are doing a work of unity. You are bringing people together. You are doing God's work.

Aristotle says that to become a friend of someone, you should eat a sack of salt together. Food and love are linked closely. Our first meal as human beings was at our mothers' breasts. We were filled with love and security and filled with nourishment. One of the worst books I have ever seen is a manual that explains how to teach people with disabilities to behave at mealtimes. Every page is about how to eat properly. When I read it I said, "They're all going to be constipated or have diarrhea!"

A meal is supposed to be a place where you can laugh, even if you get a chunk of food in your face when somebody spits on you! That's all part of the game. I am not saying we shouldn't teach good manners. That's another thing. But to make the meal a place of pedagogy is crazy. If people are tense, they risk having constipation or diarrhea. When Jesus says, "Invite them to your table," he's talking about bringing people together in friendship. And Jesus knew this wasn't always comfortable—people criticized him because he ate with sinners and prostitutes; he became their friend.

THE MYSTERY OF MEMBERSHIP

Another fundamental text for L'Arche is 1 Corinthians 12, which remains an enigma to me. It's about the body of Christ, the church, and Paul says that those parts of the body that are the weakest and least presentable are most necessary to the body and should be honored. Often the parts of the body of society that are weakest and least presentable are the ones we hide away in institutions or try to get rid of. There is today a movement for reintegration of people with learning disabilities, through work that is very positive, but we must not forget the numbers of people who still cannot work, who have psychotic behavior, who are antisocial, and who do not find acceptance and integration.

Today some people idealize people with disabilities when they find autonomy, live alone, look at television and drink beer. Autonomy can be good to a certain extent, but in our community a number of people who wanted to live alone fell into loneliness and alcoholism. The problem was not that they lived alone but that they lacked a network of friends. It always comes back to belonging. We have to discover more fully that the church is a place of compassion and fecundity, a place of welcome and friendship. We need time to listen to and understand people with communication problems. It takes time to become a friend of people with disabilities.

Before starting L'Arche I was rather serious. I prayed, I did philosophy, I taught. When I started living with people with disabilities, I learned to fool around and to celebrate life. There are three activities that are absolutely vital in the creation of community. The first is eating together around the same table. The second is praying together. And the third is celebrating together. By celebrating, I mean to laugh, to fool around, to have fun, to give thanks together for life. When we are laughing together with belly laughs, we are all the same. We're all just belly laughing. Some of our people are really crazy and really funny. They are funny because they are crazy, and they are crazy because they are funny. It's super to be with them.

In L'Arche we take every opportunity to celebrate. We celebrate birthdays. We celebrate Christmas. We have a big celebration when somebody feels called to a long-term commitment in L'Arche. We celebrate ten years, twenty years, thirty years in L'Arche. We really spend a lot of our time celebrating. And when we celebrate, we don't just give gifts. We say to one another, "You are a gift. You're a gift to the community." Around the table we can see the relationship between prayer, food and celebration. It's the place of our covenant. We are bonded together.

In my community there are about sixty assistants who have been in L'Arche more than twenty-five years. Some are married. Some are not married. There are lots of children. We know we are there for each other. Then we have all these volunteers who come and go over the years. They are super as well. We are open to each other. We laugh together. In our community there are beautiful relationships between people with disabilities. They care for each other too.

All of this takes time. For Janine, who had all that anger in her, it took years to become peaceful. What we are living is fragile. In a document he wrote about a year before he died, John Paul II said:

There is no doubt that in revealing the fundamental frailty of the human condition, the disabled person becomes an expression of the tragedy of pain. In this world of ours that approves hedonism and is charmed by ephemeral and deceptive beauty, the difficulties of the disabled are often perceived as a shame or a provocation and their problem as burdens to be removed or resolved as quickly as possible. Disabled people are instead living icons of the crucified Son. They reveal the mysterious beauty of the One who emptied himself for our sake and made himself obedient unto death. They show us over and above all appearances that the ultimate foundation of human existence is Jesus Christ. It is said justifiably so that disabled people are humanity's privileged witnesses. They can teach everyone about the love that saves us; they can become heralds of a new world, no longer dominated by force, violence, and aggression, but by love, solidarity, and acceptance—a new world transfigured by the light of Christ, the Son of God, who became incarnate, who was crucified, and rose for us.[1]

In our communities things can be going badly, and a visitor will come and say, "Oh, what peace you have in this place." Everybody sort of smiles. Somewhere it is true that there is peace. But it is so fragile. It is all a gift. Not all of it comes from our efforts. In time we learn to see and receive the gift of our life together and the peace that is there. And somehow, in the process, we are transformed.

The brothers of Taizé recently organized a pilgrimage in Bangladesh for people with disabilities, along with their families and friends, who were all from very different religious backgrounds. Afterward one of them wrote:

These days of pilgrimage of interreligious trust for the handicapped were an occasion for solidarity, for numerous discoveries, and for many a profound change of heart. The prayer and the celebration of the presence of God in the lives of handicapped people have made these days of communion a feast of hope. We discover more and more that those who are rejected by society because of their weakness and their apparent uselessness are in fact a presence of God. If we welcome them, they lead us progressively out of the world of competition and the need to do great things towards a world of communion of hearts, a life that is simple and joyful where we do small things with love. The challenge today in our country urges us on to show that the service of our weak and vulnerable brothers and sisters means opening a way of peace and unity; welcoming each other in the rich diversity of religions and cultures, serving the poor together, preparing a future of peace.

I have become very influenced by Etty Hillesum, who was assassinated at Auschwitz in 1943. At one point, when she was waiting with ten thousand Jews to be carted off, she said to God, "One thing is becoming increasingly clear to me: that you cannot help us, that we must help you to help ourselves. . . . We must help you and defend your dwelling place inside us to the last."[2] How can God come into this world if our hearts are not open to receive him so that God can be present in this world? It's somewhat similar to the words of the Apocalypse, where the Lord says, "I stand at the door and knock. The person who hears me and opens the door, I will enter and eat with that person, and that person will eat with me" (Revelation 3:20). We have to hear Jesus knocking at the door and then open the door and let him come in to be our friend. To become a friend of Jesus is to become a friend of the excluded. As we learn to be a friend of the excluded, we enter into this amazing relationship that is friendship with God.

2

Finding God in Strange Places

Why L'Arche Needs the Church

STANLEY HAUERWAS

Wat does L'Arche have to say to the church? As a theologian who looks at L'Arche and sees a miracle, this is the question with which I want to begin. The image that comes to mind in response to this question is from when I lived in South Bend, Indiana. I worshiped at Broadway Christian Parish, a United Methodist church in an area where people who worked for Studebaker had lived. When Studebaker closed its production plant, the area went downhill. It became what's called a "red line district"—an area where banks won't give loans. The church was down to about forty members, and a pastor who had come back from California was assigned to the church. As it goes with

Methodist polity, he got the absolute rear end when it came to a church placement.

John was a wonderful pastor, and he slowly helped the church to recognize the significance of frequent Eucharistic celebration. It took nine years, if you can imagine that, but we eventually moved to every-Sunday Eucharist. That was during the Reagan administration, and 25 percent of South Bend was out of work. So we decided that as part of learning what it means for God to feed us, we would feed the neighborhood. Every Sunday after church we held a neighborhood meal. We divided the church into five teams and gave the teams heady names like Charles Wesley and John Wesley. By that time we had gotten up to eighty or ninety people. Two of our members were Mrs. Camp, a very elderly lady, and her son, Gary. We never knew just what was wrong, but Gary was mentally disabled. He was high-functioning, though, and they were both very important to us.

Gary was hard of hearing, so he and Mrs. Camp sat in the front pew during services. When it came time for Eucharistic celebration, Gary would slowly help Mrs. Camp up and move to the rail. The ten-foot trip took two or three minutes, and the whole church waited with bated breath for Gary and Mrs. Camp to make it. Once they did, we all would follow. But we were led by Gary and Mrs. Camp. If they weren't present, you could feel the congregation worry whether we ought to have Eucharist that day. It wasn't clear to us that we were all gathered.

This is what I think L'Arche has to say to the church today: slow down. Just slow down. L'Arche embodies the patience that is absolutely crucial if we are to learn to be faithful people in our world. The L'Arche charter says this: "L'Arche knows that it cannot welcome everyone who has a mental handicap. It seeks to offer not a solution, but a sign that a society to be fully human must be founded on welcoming the weak and the downtrodden." Notice that L'Arche doesn't pretend to be a solution. It is a sign of hope. And hope, of course, is the way time is shaped.

Gary also read Scripture. It would take a long time. But for the church to learn to wait for the lesser member to speak in the Pauline sense is to witness to the world a different way of living in time. We live by slowing down and saying with our lives that the world will not be saved by frantic activity. If time has already been redeemed by Jesus, we learn to wait on the salvation of the Lord by taking time to listen to our weakest members.

Some years ago, when many were concerned that the Cold War might result in a nuclear holocaust, I wrote an article against the presumption that "peace" could be equated with human survival. Those who argued for peace along those lines seemed to also think that all life should be organized to ensure the elimination of nuclear weapons. We didn't have time for anything else, they said. So I wrote an article and called it "Taking Time for Peace: The Ethical Significance of the Trivial." There I argued:

Peace takes time. Put even more strongly, peace creates time by its steadfast refusal to force the other to
submit in the name of order. Peace is not a static state
but an activity which requires constant attention and
care. An activity by its very nature takes place over
time. In fact, activity creates time, as we know how
to characterize duration only by noting that we did
this first, and then this second, and so on, until we've
either gotten somewhere or accomplished this or that
task. So peace is the process through which we make
time our own rather than be determined by "events"
over which, it is alleged, we have no control.[1]

Accordingly I suggested if you want to see what peace
looks like, you need to see the work of an anthropologist
who is saving lemurs from destruction in Madagascar by
creating a colony of lemurs in North Carolina. You need to
recognize that this person is able to save lemurs because the
university gives him the time. Universities are, therefore,
not a means to peace but one of the forms peace takes—they
are peace because they explore nonviolently the conflicts we
need to have in order to discover goods in common. But
universities cannot be universities without students, which
means we have to acknowledge that the willingness of parents to offer hospitality to children (who will eventually become students) is one of the most determinative forms of
peace we have.

I don't think I had even heard of Jean Vanier when I wrote "Taking Time for Peace." But once I learned about L'Arche, I thought I saw what peace must surely look like. If I was right that the politics of peace is a politics of time, then L'Arche is surely that. For at the heart of L'Arche is patience, which is but another name for peace.[2] To join L'Arche at any level requires that you be ready to be slowed down. It is not just "all right" to take two hours to eat a meal with a core member or even longer to bathe a body not easily "handled." L'Arche requires that those who do this important work learn that time is not a zero-sum game. We have all the time we need to do what needs to be done.

A PLACE IN TIME

Patience in time is the first thing we have to learn from L'Arche. But L'Arche also teaches us the significance of place. Jean says that one of the things core members of L'Arche learn is that assistants like him aren't going away. What an extraordinary thing it is to say, "I will not leave you. You can count on me to be here day in and day out in this place." Constancy of place seems to me imperative if we are to be Christians who don't abandon one another in the name of greater goods. You cannot be constantly going and coming as an assistant at L'Arche. Core members love routines, and routines create and are created by familiarity. Familiarity is what makes place "a" place.

But place and routine can become boring without the celebration of beauty. Thus it is crucial for L'Arche that each person's birthday be celebrated in recognition of the beauty that is their life. Place and routine are transformed by recognizing the beauty of each person, which makes trust possible and thereby makes L'Arche possible. So there is a connection between structures and processes that support long-term membership in L'Arche communities and the process through which a more peaceful and just world can come into being. Without L'Arche and communities like L'Arche, we would not know what trust looks like. L'Arche reminds us how important physicality is to the habituation of place. The body becomes essential for the way we stand in relation to one another in place.

When Wolf Wolfensberger originally stated his "principle of normalization," that is, the principle that so-called disabled people were not to be treated differently simply because they were disabled, I had worries about it since I am a Texan, and Texans don't want to be normal. But then I realized that he was just saying it's important to have your dresser. It's important to have your toothbrush. Wolfensberger was just saying that how space is shaped is crucial. I suspect that we have a lot to learn from L'Arche about how space helps us care for one another through our bodies. The way L'Arche shapes time and space is important because we live in a world of speed and placelessness. This speed, as some French phenomenologists suggest, is at the very heart of the social orders we inhabit. The reason that speed and placelessness are so important has everything to do with the current trust in technology and the mobility technology makes possible—indeed, makes necessary.

Once when I was at the University of Notre Dame we had an extraordinary snowstorm. They get a lot of snow in South Bend because it's on the wrong side of the lake— every time a wind blows across Lake Michigan, the moisture gets dumped on South Bend. We were used to snow in the winter. But this particular time, we got thirty-six inches in twelve hours. It literally shut the city down. We couldn't do anything. Now, when Notre Dame was first established, it was made up of ethnic Catholics who didn't have any money. So the students did most of the work on campus. But as the students became better off and didn't want to do any work, the university increasingly hired contractors. However, this thirty-six-inch snow was so wet and heavy the workers couldn't move it with their machinery. So somebody thought it would be a good idea to ask the students to come out of the dorms and clean the sidewalks. They announced over the student radio station, "Come to the student union and help us clean the sidewalks." Only they forgot the students would need shovels. People started looking around and discovered there were only five snow shovels on all of Notre Dame's campus. We had used mechanical snow removers for so long, we couldn't just go back to the old way.

I remember thinking, *When technology replaces community, you ain't got community to fall back on when you're in a crisis.*

That seems to me to be an image of how speed has produced technology, which then undercuts the viability of community. We see it in medicine today; the task is not to care for patients but to cure them. When caring turns into curing, we don't know what to do with patients when we can't cure them. What do we do with people who have diseases it seems they won't recover from? That's speed taking over.

Speed also has to do with politics—in particular, war. According to Paul Virilio, the dominant form violence takes in modernity is speed. He says that contemporary war is shaped by mechanisms of mass communication, which makes war less about territory and more about information management. As a result, our perceptions are mediated by logics of violence—speed creates a new vision of the world in which everyone "naturally" understands himself or herself to be part of the war machine. Local space and time disappear and are replaced by a single, global, virtual "real time." This, according to Virilio, is "what the doctrine of security is founded on: the saturation of time and space by speed, making daily life the last theater of operations, the ultimate scene of strategic foresight."[3]

Just as we try to cure all illness, we use war to make ourselves think that the world can be made safe. So war becomes the way to peace, which obviously produces more war. The alleged democracies in which we live run on speed, necessitating technologies designed to help us become the sort of people who do not need anyone. It seems to me that democracies want to produce people who do not need to rely on trusting one another.

I love the Isle of Mull in Scotland—for one, it is beautiful. But I also love the roads on Mull. They are all single-lane with a pullover about every five hundred yards. Driving on those roads is a constant negotiation; you see a car coming and you have to make a judgment about who should pull off first. To drive on Mull requires constant cooperative trust. I think it makes a difference for the whole community. If you stay on Mull for a while, you discover that everybody knows one another. They have a sense of one another's strengths and weaknesses. That's exactly what we try to plan out of our lives today—that kind of cooperative relationship.

HUMANISM GONE BAD

The understanding of time and place that L'Arche represents, which is a challenge to the speed and placelessness of modernity, helps us understand part of the problem we face as the church today. Having lost the power and status we had in societies we thought we had Christianized, we Christians now find ourselves most often on the wrong side of the "progressive" forces of human history. In response, many Christians want to identify with the alleged humanisms produced by speed and placelessness. So the church finds herself saying constantly, "Oh, yes, we support that too! Oh, yes, we think these developments are wonderful."

Who can be against knowing more and more about the genome in order to help us become well before we become sick? It's a deep temptation for the church to say, "Hey, we're on the side of historical progress, too!"

Of course, if you say that L'Arche knows it cannot welcome everyone who has a mental handicap and seeks to offer not a solution but a sign, that doesn't sound like good news in a world built on speed and placelessness. The question then becomes, "Well, does that mean you are against trying to cure cancer?" After all, "progress" we assume means eliminating what threatens to kill us or at least slow us down. But you can cure cancer without eliminating the patient. You cannot "cure" the mentally handicapped without eliminating the patient. L'Arche stands as a reminder that "progress" should not mean eliminating all that threatens us. After all, even if you cure cancer, you are going to die of some other ailment. L'Arche dares in the face of death and by so doing transforms what we mean by "progress."

Modernity gets us caught up in some funny contradictions. For example, in the United States we now spend between 15 and 17 percent of the gross national product on crisis-care medicine, which of course has nothing to do with the health of the population. If we're interested in the health of the population, the most important things to focus on are windows, sewers and good nutrition. Crisis-care medicine is not going to keep us alive. It may keep someone alive another six months or a year, but it won't necessarily improve the health of the population. But we are spending 16 percent of the gross national product on crisis-care medicine. Sixty percent of that goes to people in their last year of life. It's interesting how the medical imperative presumes that if we can do it, we have to do it. The way we show we love Mom is to make sure she gets every possible treatment, which may be another form of torture in the end.

This relates to the presumption that people should not have children if they've been diagnosed with a mental disability —that abortion is the appropriate response. I think that presumption is based on our understanding of compassion; it is humanism gone mad. We have to be careful what we mean when we say "humanity." Christian humanism is determined by the Father's sending of the Son to be one of us. So humanism must always begin with Jesus' humanity. When that isn't the case, then in a world of speed and placelessness, compassion becomes a way to say certain people would be better off dead.

When I was active in the Association of Retarded Citizens (now known as The Arc), I would go into the Cardinal Nursing Home in South Bend, Indiana, and see fifty people in the day room. Their clothes were stripped off, and they were often sitting in their own feces. That place was designed, I'm afraid, to produce in visitors the reaction, "These people would be better off dead." If you took those same people and put them in a residential home with people who cared about them, you might want to have a meal there. Compassion can go crazy in an environment of what looks like necessity. If the church becomes identified with the world of speed and placelessness in the name of humanism and compassion, it seems to me that we will live in a world in which L'Arche cannot help but be seen as a reactionary form of life. But that means that L'Arche is a prophetic sign of what the church needs to see if we are to avoid the world of speed and placelessness.

Along these lines, the church can be tempted to underwrite a kind of universalism that confuses what it means to be catholic with what it means to be part of a "common humanity." Before we had the word *global*, we Christians had another word: *catholic*. This word means that real people are connected with other real people through the office of the bishop. What we have in common isn't an idea but stories. And I cannot tell my story well unless I also hear your story. The office of the bishop is to make sure that churches in their locality do not become isolated from the stories of other churches in their locality. In our particularity we may get some things wrong, and we constantly have to be tested. It takes time. But that's the catholicity that Christians represent. It is quite different from the universalism represented by the high humanism embodied in speed and placelessness.

A MODEST PROPOSAL

L'Arche is the reality at the heart of the church insofar as it reminds us that we have all the time we need in the world in a world of the deepest injustice to care for one another. People right now are dying of hunger, and you are sitting and reading a book. (I, more likely than not, am sitting and writing another one.) We have time for this not because we choose to ignore the poor, but because we believe there is a faithful and an unfaithful way to feed the poor. And it is worth our time to try to name that. I believe L'Arche is the place where God has made it possible for Christians to learn to be hope in a world where there is no solution. As we say in Texas, that's "hard learning."

I have often said that Christians are called to nonviolence not because we believe nonviolence is a strategy to rid the world of war—though we certainly want to rid the world of war. Rather, as faithful followers of Christ in a world at war, we cannot imagine being anything other than nonviolent. Of course we want to make war less likely. But nonviolence is a sign of hope that there is an alternative to war. And that alternative is called church.

I have on my office door a sign from the Mennonite Central Committee that shows two anguished people embracing one another. Below the picture is a slogan that says, "A modest proposal for peace: let the Christians of the world resolve not to kill one another." I have people knock on my door all the time and say, "That makes me so mad." I say, "Really? Why?" They say, "Well, Christians shouldn't kill anyone." And I say, "They call it a modest proposal. You've got to begin somewhere."

L'Arche is a modest proposal. You've got to begin somewhere. And we must remember that if the account I have given of nonviolence is true, it may well make the world more violent. After all, the world does not want the lies called "order" to be confused with peace. So Christian commitment to nonviolence will be extraordinarily conflictual. The gentleness of L'Arche has not yet produced significant enemies. It will be interesting to see how long that will last. We will see what kind of enemies it can produce.

In a world determined to cure those who cannot be cured, Christians should refuse to do anything other than be with those Jesus taught us to be loved by—that is, those we "help" by simply being present. Miners used to carry canaries with them into the mines because a canary dies more quickly from methane gas than a human does. Since methane has no smell, the miners knew to get out of the mine only when they saw the canary keel over. I think L'Arche may be the church's canary. By watching L'Arche, we know when we face the "culture of death," in John Paul II's language. Accordingly, I think L'Arche forces us to be faithful. If we must say, "Those people are us!" then, as a matter of fact, that's forcing ourselves to be faithful. We can rarely will ourselves to be faithful. It's usually a necessity that we find we cannot avoid.

That's what I think L'Arche has to say to the church. It offers a kind of time, a kind of patience, and a kind of placedness that comes from faithfulness and produces a different understanding of catholicity. That is how L'Arche helps the church find the gospel.

But L'Arche also needs the church. Its charter states, "Each community maintains links with appropriate authorities. Its members are integrated with local churches and other places of worship." L'Arche is not the church. Because it is so compelling and gives us something worth doing in a world with so few examples of what's worth doing, L'Arche is almost overwhelming. Lives are so taken up in it that members can think they don't need to worship God with other Christians who are not at L'Arche.

L'Arche is similar to some of early monasticism. It has a very strong monastic foundation. Of course, monasticism is where reform always comes from in the church. It is also distrusted by the church because it is filled with people who would reform it. That's just the sort of tension a gift like L'Arche creates.

I have a great deal of appreciation for John Paul II, but one of his phrases that I disliked was, "The family is the domestic church." I thought, *How horrible. The only possible reason we can sustain families is that they're not the church.* Families are a threat to the church to the extent that they create loyalties more determinative than our loyalty to the church. In the same way, I think L'Arche needs the wider church exactly to the extent it can become too significant.

L'Arche needs the wider church because its members need to leave L'Arche to worship God elsewhere, in another place, with all the time and bother that may require. This is not just for the sake of the people within L'Arche, but for the sake of the church. L'Arche must remain connected with other modes of Christian life that make L'Arche possible. The body of L'Arche must always be integrated into the larger body of Christ through interconnectedness with other communities around the world.

3

The Vision of Jesus

Living Peaceably in a Wounded World

JEAN VANIER

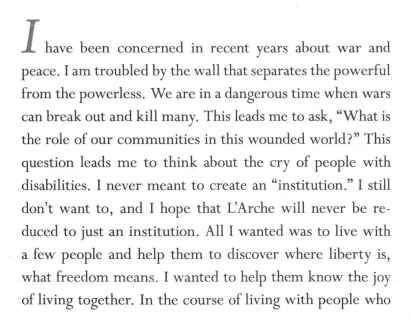

I have been concerned in recent years about war and peace. I am troubled by the wall that separates the powerful from the powerless. We are in a dangerous time when wars can break out and kill many. This leads me to ask, "What is the role of our communities in this wounded world?" This question leads me to think about the cry of people with disabilities. I never meant to create an "institution." I still don't want to, and I hope that L'Arche will never be reduced to just an institution. All I wanted was to live with a few people and help them to discover where liberty is, what freedom means. I wanted to help them know the joy of living together. In the course of living with people who are disabled, I have learned to listen to their cry. I wanted to accept all the implications that that carried, and to work in collaboration with local authorities.

In the Gospels we are confronted by the story of Lazarus and the rich man. When I tell that parable of Lazarus and the rich man, people can feel a little bit awkward. A few years ago I had the joy of speaking to the beggars and tramps in Burkina Faso, where we have a community. I was invited to a little hangar where the beggars would congregate, and I said to myself, "My God, what can I talk to these guys about?" It became obvious that I had to talk to them about Lazarus. Many of them were Muslims, some were Christians, and others were of African religions. When you say that Lazarus was found in the bosom of Abraham, Muslims understand that. So I said to them, "You guys, you are Lazarus!" And they were so happy. They started clapping their hands. They were excited. When I tell that parable in the rich parishes of Paris, people are not quite so excited! It makes one wonder, whose side are we on?

I remember being in Chile, going along a road from the airport. My driver told me, "Oh, here on the right are all the rich houses, and here on the left are the slums. And nobody crosses over this road." We live in an incredibly wounded world. I don't want to give the impression that there are goodies and baddies and that we can issue a moral judgment. We all know that within the slum areas there are incredibly beautiful men and women—incredibly beautiful mothers and fathers who are struggling against a drug culture. Likewise, on the other side of the road in the rich areas, there are incredibly beautiful people. It's not as simple as good people versus bad people. That road was like a wall. Within each of us there is also a wall.

WALLS OF FEAR

I would like to talk a little bit about these walls that divide humanity. And I want to begin with a little word from Genesis 3. Adam has just broken off from God. As always when we break off from God, after a while God runs after us. God says, "Adam, where are you?" Adam replies, "I was frightened because I was naked, and so I hid."

Three words: fear, nakedness and hiding. What are we afraid of? We had a meeting in my community not too long ago where we talked about fear. Everyone was asked to talk about their fundamental fear in some way. What were they most afraid of? Different words came out: *rejection, abandonment, not succeeding, failure, deterioration, death.* When you look at all these kinds of fear, the common denominator is always the fear of being pushed down or being seen as valueless or nonexistent. Once we name the fear that is deep inside of us, we can begin to identify the compulsion that protects us from being pushed down. We begin to see why we can become obsessed with having a name where we can be glorified, or achieving a position where we can be seen as worthy.

A friend of mine is a chaplain in a prison in Cleveland. One of the inmates came up to him and asked, "Do you like preaching?"

"Yeah," my friend said, "I do enjoy preaching."

"Do you preach well?" this inmate asked.

"Yes, I think so," my friend replied.

"Well," continued the inmate, "I am the best car thief in Cleveland, and I like it!" He had found his compulsion. He was the best. Isn't that what all of us are looking for—to be the best? It's important to also know what our fears are and to name our compulsions.

The walls that separate people who are frightened of disabilities from those who have disabilities exist everywhere. There is no meeting between them. A friend of mine who was working with people in the world of prostitution said to me, "If you dare to listen to their stories, you will be changed." Another person in L'Arche in Australia was working with people in the world of prostitution, and she had been walking with a particular young man for quite some time. One day she was going through a park in Sydney and found him dying of an overdose. As she knelt beside him, he said to her, "You have always wanted to change me. You have never accepted me as I am." Can we accept and love people with disabilities as they are?

When we want to change people, we have power. We have generosity. We have goodness. But we create a cleavage when we want to do good things for people.

The vision of Jesus was extraordinary. He appeared on this earth in a world filled with immense hatred and warfare. Peace was being imposed by the armies of Rome—the great Pax Romana. But there was conflict everywhere. We live in a world where groups close up, thinking that they and their traditions are the best. They oppose others, either to bring them to the so-called truth or to take more land. It's the reality of history. Jesus entered into this world to love people as they are.

The heart of the vision of Jesus is to bring people together, to meet, to engage in dialogue, to love each other. Jesus wants to break down the walls that separate people and groups. How will he do this? He will do it by saying to each one, "You are important. You are precious." There can be no peacemaking or social work or anything else to improve our world unless we are convinced that the other is important. You are precious. *You*—not just "people," but you. And we have a call to make history, not just accept history. We are called to change things—to change the movement of history, to make our world a place of love and not just a place of conflict and competition.

WEAKNESS AS THE WAY TO GOD

Living in L'Arche I have learned that it is a revelation for people with disabilities if you say to them, "There is meaning to your life." We are not just doing good to them as professionals. That is important, but it's not just about that. It's about revealing to them that they have value. They have something to say to our society. In some mysterious way, they are calling to me, to us all, to change. I spoke some time ago in Aleppo in Syria, mainly to the Muslim community, and there was a mufti there who has since become the great mufti of Syria. When I finished he got up and said, "If I have understood well, people with disabilities lead us to God."

We are afraid of showing weakness. We are afraid of not succeeding. Deep inside we are afraid of not being recognized. So we pretend we are the best. We hide behind power. We hide behind all sorts of things. However, when we meet people with disabilities and reveal to them through our eyes and ears and words that they are precious, they are changed. But we too are changed. We are led to God.

Shortly after the genocide in Rwanda, I met with people from the Faith and Light communities there. They came from the villages, and we had a beautiful little retreat in the cathedral of Butare. During a very moving moment, many mothers of children with severe disabilities came forward during the celebration of the Eucharist and lifted their children up as a gift to God.

Later, we had a meeting with all these women. I asked, "What has Faith and Light brought to you?" And they said, "We no longer feel ashamed." When we read Deuteronomy 28, we see that at the heart of the Jewish vision is the belief that disability and sickness are caused by sin. A son with a disability reveals that somewhere in yourself and your family you are doing things against God, against truth and against love. This vision is frighteningly powerful. That is why in the ninth chapter of John the immediate question the disciples ask Jesus when they see a man born blind is, "Is it because he has sinned or because his parents have sinned?" Jesus answers, "Neither he nor his parents have sinned, but it is so that the work of God may be manifested in him."

In some countries that I have visited, the pain of mothers is multiplied because their husbands abandon them, considering the child's disability to be the fault of the mother. In some places, to look after people with disabilities means you are favoring situations that are wrong. People say you should just leave the disabled alone in their pain. There is a sort of mystery about people with disabilities. What is their meaning in our world? Is it a malediction or a benediction?

Francoise came to our community nearly thirty years ago. She walked only a little and couldn't eat by herself. She had a severe learning disability. She is now about seventy-five, older and weaker. She has become blind and lives in a little home where there are ten people with severe multiple disabilities. Francoise is really quite beautiful. What touches me is how the assistants wash her and prepare food for her. But she can't see the way they prepare the food and feed her, and I ask myself, "What is the mystery behind this woman of seventy-five who cannot leave her bed and who cries out now and again?" The assistants say, "She is our mama, our little grandmother."

They love her with tenderness and gentleness. What is the meaning of this mystery of people with severe disabilities?

I know a man who lives in Paris. His wife has Alzheimer's. He was an important businessman—his life filled with busyness. But he said that when his wife fell sick, "I just couldn't put her into an institution, so I keep her. I feed her. I bathe her." I went to Paris to visit them, and this businessman who had been very busy all his life said, "I have changed. I have become more human." I got a letter from him recently. He said that in the middle of the night his wife woke him up. She came out of the fog for a moment, and she said, "Darling, I just want to say thank you for all you're doing for me." Then she fell back into the fog. He said, "I wept and I wept."

It all sounds so crazy. But when something is totally crazy, it may be that we have to go deeper. There's a mystery, and maybe it comes back to the question of who God is and where God is. This was a big question during the Shoah, when the Jewish people had to ask, "Where is God?" Where is God in all the places of pain? We don't want to look at all this messy world of the mafia, corruption, prostitution and slavery. This is a world of terrible pain, and it is clear that we can be very frightened of it. We begin to understand Lazarus and the rich man. The rich man doesn't want to contact Lazarus because if he did he would have to change. It's like that man who works with people in prostitution. He says, "Now that I have listened to their stories, I will never be the same."

WE CAN DO NOTHING ON OUR OWN

When we listen to stories of terrible pain and know we can't do anything about it, we touch our own vulnerability. We have heard the scream of pain, but we don't know what to do with it. None of us knows what to do with the deep brokenness of our world. Maybe that realization can bring us back to community. We can do nothing on our own. We need somewhere to be together.

I recently came across some very strong words by Martin Luther King Jr. He said something like this: "How hard it is for people to live without someone to look down upon—really to look down upon. It is not just that they feel cheated out of someone to hate. It is that they are compelled to look more closely into themselves and what they don't like in themselves." It's obvious that we are all a mixture of light and darkness; we have all touched the places of hypocrisy and lies. All of us have felt that tendency to want to prove that we are better than others, to go up the ladder, to be respected—even in L'Arche. Anywhere.

But as we live with people who have been crushed, as we begin to welcome the stranger, we will gradually discover the stranger inside of us. When we welcome the broken outside, they call us to discover the broken inside. We cannot really enter into relationship with people who are broken unless somehow we deal with our own brokenness. I am not saying that we all have to go through psychotherapy. But what are we hiding? Or what are we hiding behind? We must discern our natural inner protectiveness and compulsive attitudes. Somewhere we are hiding our weaknesses.

And yet weakness is an important part of our reality. We were born weak. We needed unconditional love. We needed our mums to say, "You're more beautiful than I expected," or "It's good that you exist; you are unique." One of our assistants reported that she'd heard a mother say to her child, "I would have aborted you if I could." Memories like this are very deep in the hearts of people, just as they are in children who were abused sexually. They can produce a fundamental breakage. We all have a deep fear of our own weaknesses because my weakness is what makes it possible for someone else to crush me. So I create mechanisms of defense and compulsion to protect myself. We all have protective systems designed to prevent people from seeing who we are.

While weakness can be beautiful, it can also be terribly dangerous. I can understand the immense pain of parents. Recently a father asked me to go and see his wife. She was forty years old and eight months pregnant. She was in tears and a bit hysterical—this was her first baby and she knew that the child had a disability. I saw immediately that I couldn't say a word to her. There are times when you must not say nice words. What I could do was send her to visit another mother who'd had a child a year previously with similar disabilities to the child she was going to have. The two women got together and wept.

Today in France they are saying that within a few years there will be no more children with Down syndrome because they will all have been aborted. I go into schools and I hear kids saying, "If I have a monster within me, I will get rid of it." That reality is there. Of course, if the mother sees the child as a terrible disappointment, then the child feels that he or she is a disappointment. It's not easy for a child to feel this. Deep down, the self-image of the child is broken. The child feels, "I am no good."

The heart of L'Arche is to say to people, "I am glad you exist." And the proof that we are glad that they exist is that we stay with them for a long time. We are together, we can have fun together. "I am glad you exist" is translated into physical presence.

HOW JESUS BRINGS PEOPLE TOGETHER

We live in a world of immense pain. We have to ask what it all means, who we are within it and, most importantly, how to break through our systems of protection. I've already said that Jesus has a vision—a very deep vision—for how to overcome our divisions. Knowing something about history helps us to see the vision more clearly. People with disabilities, particularly the lepers, were totally rejected in Jesus' day. Strong social barriers stood between the Jewish people and the Romans. The world was broken up into little groups defined by the Romans as it had been by the Greeks before them. This is the way of empires. There used to be a British empire, now there's an American empire and soon there will be a Chinese one. So the world goes on. Empires rise and fall. They want to dominate the world by imposing their "peace" on it.

The Word became flesh to bring people together, to break down the walls of fear and hatred that separate people. That's the vision of the incarnation—to bring people together. In his prayer for unity Jesus prayed that we might all become one. We have this incredible vision of peacemaking, two thousand years in the making. There may be another fifty thousand years left to go. I don't know. But Christ is always working to bring people together. The danger is what Martin Luther King Jr. said: we have this tendency to push some people down so that we can rise up.

I read an interesting remark in a book by a French economist who asked the question, How is it that after all these years of immense technology there are still millions of people who have no fresh water? How is it that they are without enough food, or adequate medical help for all those who have AIDS, particularly in Africa? We never seem to be able to do anything about this poverty except send a little bit of money. Poverty is continually there, that vast wall. This economist says, "I don't think we can eradicate this terrible poverty because of our consciousness of death." We have to prove that we are better than our neighbor. We have to show that we have more than others—more power, more wealth, more goodness. Once the situation of workers in the United Kingdom and France was more or less resolved through just hours and just pay, then people from other countries were brought in to do the jobs others didn't want to do. There is always a need for a poorer person just to show that I am better off.[1]

We are all going to die one day. We will all become poor eventually. Why worry about being better than others when we will eventually understand that we are all part of one humanity on the day we are put under the ground and the tombstone is placed over us? A few years later the tombstone may be taken away and we will be forgotten altogether.

Our reality is one of division and of fear of weakness and death. But somewhere in our hearts there is a desire for peace. The vision of Jesus is that we meet people at the bottom and help bring them up to trust themselves. In order to break down the walls that separate people we must not hit the walls. We must begin at the bottom. Jesus came to announce good news to the poor, freedom to captives, liberty to the oppressed, sight to the blind. Let's help the poor to rise up, and then help those who have power and money to see that for the sake of peace, which is the greatest good human beings can seek, they too should enter into this vision and start helping the weak to rise up.

When this happens, everyone will begin to change. Those who have power and riches will start to become more humble, and those who are rising up will leave behind their need to be victims, their need to be angry or depressed. This spirituality will say that God wants me to be where I am, as I am, and humble. This is the spirituality of life, which helps people stand up and take their place. It is not a spirituality of death. Jesus wants those who have been crushed to rise up and those who have power to discover that there is another road—a road of sharing and of compassion.

JESUS LOVES ME AS I AM

There was a little boy with a disability who was making his first Communion in a church in Paris. After the liturgy a family celebration of tea and coffee took place. The little boy's uncle went over to the mother and said, "Wasn't it a beautiful liturgy? The only sad part is that he didn't understand anything." The little boy heard and with tears in his eyes said, "Don't worry, Mummy, Jesus loves me as I am."

It's OK just to be myself. If I am getting older, that's OK. That's who I am. It's part of my journey. I don't have to be what others want me to be. But our society doesn't affirm who we are, so we struggle with our identity. During the football (soccer) season everybody, whether English or French or Italian, screams with joy or bursts into tears because they want their own side to win. We have our cultural identity, our religious identity—or our irreligious identity. When we are governed by our national or ethnic identity, we quickly fall into rivalry. To avoid a rivalry that can turn to hate, we need to discover something more fundamental.

This is what Jesus wants to give us—a fundamental identity of truthfulness. Jesus wants us to become friends of truth. He wants us to have an identity like that little boy— a consciousness of being loved by him. If we develop that which is most intimate in us, we are transformed. We no longer seek glory from the group; instead we become free. That is transformation.

We are called to meet people just as they are and to know that each one is precious and important. Of course, some people act as enemies or terrorists. We can have many hurts in our hearts. But the real question is always how to discover our fundamental identity as children of God who are united to all others with the same fundamental identity. As we discover this, we find ways to meet one another and dialogue one with another.

The vision Jesus came to share is about meeting people and trusting people. Faith in Jesus is trust that we are loved. It is knowing that deeper than being part of a group, religious or otherwise, there is the fundamental experience of becoming a friend of truth, a friend of Jesus, a friend of God. But I can't do this alone. I need community. I need friends.

Over the last forty years I have learned the transforming power of people with disabilities. I don't live all the time in a home anymore. I have a little place outside. But I have the privilege of eating all my meals in a home with people with disabilities. I realize as I get older that I have difficulty meeting so-called normal people. I don't know what to talk about with them. But I can fool around at the dinner table with people with disabilities. I see that I am becoming a bit marginalized. I know that it is important to speak to the wider world, but it is not always easy to live in two worlds. In the wider world I speak about the people in my home and the fun we have. I talk about discovering that the important thing is to be with people with disabilities, to rejoice with them, to celebrate life and have fun. A lot of people know how to drink whisky and go to the cinemas, but they don't know how to celebrate. To celebrate is to say we are happy together.

Jesus came to change a world in which those at the top have privilege, power, prestige and money while those at the bottom are seen as useless. Jesus came to create a body. Paul, in 1 Corinthians 12, compares the human body to the body of Christ, and he says that those parts of the body that are the weakest and least presentable are indispensable to the body. In other words, people who are the weakest and least presentable are indispensable to the church. I have never seen this as the first line of a book on ecclesiology. Who really believes it? But this is the heart of faith, of what it means to be the church. Do we really believe that the weakest, the least presentable, those we hide away—that they are indispensable? If that was our vision of the church, it would change many things.

I have been trying to point out that our deep need is to meet those on the other side of the wall, to discover their gifts, to appreciate them. We must not get caught up in the need for power over the poor. We need to be with the poor. That can seem a bit crazy because it doesn't look like a plan to change the world. But maybe we will change the world if we are happy. Maybe what we need most is to rejoice and to celebrate with the weak and the vulnerable. Maybe the most important thing is to learn how to build communities of celebration. Maybe the world will be transformed when we learn to have fun together. I don't mean to suggest that we don't talk about serious things. But maybe what our world needs more than anything is communities where we celebrate life together and become a sign of hope for our world. Maybe we need signs that it is possible to love each other.

4

The Politics of Gentleness

STANLEY HAUERWAS

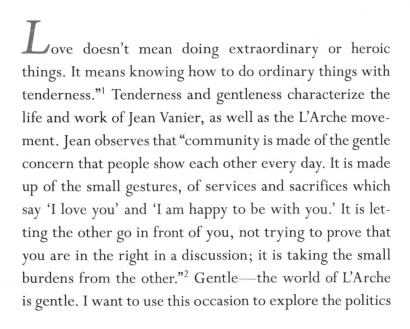

*L*ove doesn't mean doing extraordinary or heroic things. It means knowing how to do ordinary things with tenderness."[1] Tenderness and gentleness characterize the life and work of Jean Vanier, as well as the L'Arche movement. Jean observes that "community is made of the gentle concern that people show each other every day. It is made up of the small gestures, of services and sacrifices which say 'I love you' and 'I am happy to be with you.' It is letting the other go in front of you, not trying to prove that you are in the right in a discussion; it is taking the small burdens from the other."[2] Gentle—the world of L'Arche is gentle. I want to use this occasion to explore the politics of gentleness. Why must gentleness be part of any politics that would be just?

Gentleness is usually the last thing most of us would associate with the rough-and-tumble world of politics. Politics, we assume, is about conflict and getting interests satisfied. Gentleness, on the other hand, is a characteristic of personal relationships. It has little to do with questions of power or rule. That is, of course, exactly the dichotomy I want to challenge by calling attention to the role of gentleness in L'Arche.

I want to draw on Jean and the work of L'Arche to develop a critique of contemporary assumptions about ethics and politics. So I am "using" Vanier and his friends, but I am not going to apologize for writing about the intellectually disabled. For those of us in the universities who don't live with the disabled every day, it feels like something of a fraud to use people with disabilities to make a point. But I am going to make the most from being drawn into the world of L'Arche and try as best I can to say why L'Arche has so much to teach us.

To focus on gentleness does create a rhetorical problem, though. My style is polemical and many, I suspect, would not characterize my work as gentle or tender. Accordingly, I worry that my attempt to argue for the significance of gentleness for Jean and L'Arche may betray what he and L'Arche are about. My only defense is that God has given us different tasks. My task has been to put Vanier's wisdom into conversation with philosophical and political positions that I fear are antithetical—if not outright threats—to the people we call "intellectually disabled." That means, however, that my writing style has been aggressive and confrontational.

However, I do not want the way I argue to belie the significance of gentleness. I hope I will prove to be an adequate listener, because learning to listen is basic to the gentle character of life in L'Arche. But I am an academic, and academics are notoriously bad listeners. We always think we know what people are going to say before they say it, and we have a response to what we thought they would say in spite of what they may have actually said. To learn to listen well, it turns out, may require learning to be a gentle person.

That is particularly true if Jean is right that to learn to listen can be quite painful. For example, Jean has written,

Communities which start by serving the poor must gradually discover the gifts that those poor people bring. The communities start in generosity; they must grow to listen. In the end, the most important thing is not to do things for people who are poor and in distress, but to help them to have confidence in themselves. . . . Some communities grow by listening to their members' needs for formation and well-being. This growth is usually material: the communities go for the best and most comfortable buildings, where everyone has their own room. These communities will die fairly quickly. Other communities will grow by listening to the cry of the poor. Most of the time, this leads them to become poorer themselves, so that they can be closer to poor people.[3]

What might that mean, if I am to listen to Jean? I do not want to become poorer. I want to remain the academic who can pretend to defend those with mental disabilities by being more articulate than those I am criticizing. In short, I do not want to learn to be gentle. I want to be a warrior on behalf of L'Arche, doing battle against the politics that threaten to destroy these gentle communities. Jean, of course, is no less a warrior. But where I see an enemy to be defeated, he sees a wound that needs to be healed. That's a deep difference.

According to Jean, we all carry a deep wound—the wound of our loneliness. That is why we find it hard to be alone, and we try to heal our aloneness by joining a community. But to belong for the sake of belonging cannot help but lead to disappointment. We must realize, as Jean says, that "this wound is inherent in the human condition and that what we have to do is walk with it instead of fleeing from it. We cannot accept it until we discover that we are loved by God just as we are, and that the Holy Spirit, in a mysterious way, is living at the centre of the wound."[4]

This is the radical insight at the heart of L'Arche. Until we learn to see our enemies as wounded people who are loved by God, gentleness is not possible. The stories Jean tells of the disabled are often stories of loneliness not easily overcome. For example, he tells the story of Daniel, whose disabilities were so severe his parents did not want him. After being put in one institution after another, Daniel ended up in a psychiatric hospital. Jean observes that even at L'Arche Daniel would now and again flip out of reality, "hiding his anguish and himself behind hallucinations. He had constructed thick walls around his heart that prevented him from being who he was. He felt guilty for existing, because nobody wanted him as he was."[5] Jean notes, as he did in the last chapter, that the heart of a child is easily hurt, and the hurt becomes a wound around which we build walls of protection. Walls so constructed can be breached only by gentleness.

THE POLITICS OF GENTLENESS

But what does this have to do with politics? I think the gentleness of L'Arche helps us see why liberal political theory has found it difficult to provide moral standing for people with mental disabilities. I need to be clear that when I say "liberal political theory," I'm not talking about the ideas behind the platform of America's Democratic party. I am referring, instead, to the political philosophy that both liberals and conservatives in America assume. According to Hans Reinders, at the heart of our political arrangements is the assumption that "individuals are free to live their own

lives as they prefer, provided that they allow other people
equal freedom to do the same, and provided that they accept and receive a fair share of the burden and benefits of
the social cooperation."[6]

My way of putting this more colloquially is to say that
we live in a time when people believe they have no story
except the story they chose when they thought they had
no story. That's "freedom" in a society shaped by liberal
political theory. If you don't believe that's true of you,
just ask yourself whether you believe someone should be
held responsible for a decision they made when they didn't
know what they were doing. Most of us don't; this ethos
of freedom is deep in our souls. We believe we should be
held responsible only for the things we freely chose when
we knew what we were doing.

The problem with this way of thinking is that it makes
marriage unintelligible. How do we ever know what we
are doing when we promise lifelong monogamous fidel-
ity? Christians are required to marry before witnesses in
church so we can hold them to the promises they made
when they didn't know what they were doing. If marriage renders this understanding of freedom unintelligible, try having children. You never get the ones you
wanted. Yet we still feel extraordinary pressure to raise
our children in such a way that they will not have to suffer for our convictions. Otherwise, we think they would
not be "free." But this just reveals that we do not know

why we're having children. And this has everything to do with the deep assumptions about freedom that now shape our lives. We believe that we should produce people who have no story except the story they chose when they had no story. So our children grow up thinking that freedom is the choice between a Sony and a Panasonic.

In a culture that understands freedom this way, Reinders says we assume that people with mental disabilities lack

> to a greater or lesser extent the powers of reason and free will. Since these are powers that bring substance to the core values of the liberal view of public moral-ity, mentally disabled people never acquire full moral standing in this view. This is because its moral com-munity is constituted by "persons" and these, in turn, are constituted by the powers of reason and free will. This conception of the person is particularly problem-atic with respect to the inclusion of severely mentally disabled citizens, since on the liberal view only per-sons in the sense of rational moral agents can be recipi-ents of equal concern and respect.[7]

I fear it may sound overdramatic, but what Reinders de-scribes is what I take to be the wound that drives contem-porary politics—a wound, moreover, that is well protected by walls not easily breached because they seem so reason-able. The myth of freedom I described above is the story we tell ourselves to hide the fact that we are not, indeed, our own creatures. Some of the work being done in political philosophy supports my point here. In the latter half of the last century, no political philosopher was more influential than John Rawls, who wrote the now-classic book *A Theory of Justice*. Martha Nussbaum, one of America's most prominent public intellectuals, is an heir of Rawls. Nussbaum has acknowledged that liberal political theory has difficulty recognizing the status of the mentally disabled. In her book *Frontiers of Justice: Disability, Nationality, Species Membership*, Nussbaum observes that the people we assume capable of participating in a just society "are human beings possessed of no serious mental or physical impairments."[8]

Rather than abandon the dominant understanding of politics, Nussbaum wants to remedy liberal political theory to include the disabled without abandoning the fundamental insights of liberalism. She does this in the name of three mentally disabled people: Sesha, the daughter of philosopher Eva Kittay and her husband Jeffrey, who will never walk, talk or read because of her cerebral palsy and mental retardation; Nussbaum's nephew, Arthur, who is without any social skills due to Asperger's syndrome and who is unable to learn in school but is mechanically adept; and Jamie Berube, who was born with Down syndrome and is the son of literary critics Michael Berube and Janet Lyon.[9] Even though these are all the children of academics, Nussbaum does name real people. This is not just a theoretical exercise for her.

According to Nussbaum, the attempt to secure social cooperation on the basis of mutual advantage for the contracting parties is at the heart of liberal political theory. A "strong rationalism," as she calls it, informs the liberal project in the hope that an account of political life that avoids appeals to intuitions and prejudices can be justified.[10] One of the aspects of liberal political theory is an attempt to avoid contingency. We try to give an argument that is true without appealing to our experience in contingent historical conditions. Liberalism teaches us to provide an account of justice that does not depend on the presumption of altruism, but rather assumes an admittedly fictive bargaining process that establishes fundamental principles of mutual advantage. The presumption is that people will do the right things if they can see that it really is in their best interest.

Nussbaum does not call into question these fundamental presuppositions of the liberal political project. Yet she acknowledges that this understanding of justice has omitted people of disability from consideration. This is at least partly the result of not distinguishing the question "By whom are society's basic principles designed?" from the question "For whom are society's basic principles designed?"[11] She thinks we have conflated the questions "By whom?" and "For whom?" Because of this confusion, Nussbaum says, liberal political theory ends with a counterintuitive result because those with mental disability are excluded. Such a result is counterintuitive because, at least in our time, the issue of justice for people with disabilities is prominent on the agenda of every decent society, the omission of all of them from participation in the situation of basic political choice looks problematic, given the evident capacity of many if not all of them for choice; and their omission from the group of persons for whom society's most basic principles are chosen is more problematic still.[12]

The tension Nussbaum is struggling with is this ambiguous position of our society: at the same time that we say we want to take care of the disabled among us, we also want to eliminate them. It would seem that all Rawls (or other like-minded liberal theorists) need do to respond to Nussbaum's concern for the disabled is to acknowledge that some provision needs to be made for people who are disabled when they come to the bargaining table to negotiate their self-interest. You might say we can have a fair game if we just level the playing field at the start. But Rawls is unable to accept this suggestion, Nussbaum argues, because if he did so, he "would lose a simple and straightforward way of measuring who is the least well-off in society, a determination that he needs to make for purposes of thinking about material distribution and redistribution, and which he makes with reference to income and wealth alone."[13]

So Nussbaum thinks that rather than focusing on income and wealth as Rawls does, a capabilities approach is necessary if the mentally disabled are not to be unfairly excluded. We have to learn to ask, "What is each person capable of doing?" According to Nussbaum, to focus on capabilities means that we are fundamentally bodily beings whose rationality is but one aspect of our animality. Therefore our "bodily need, including our need for care, is a feature of our rationality and our sociability."[14] To focus on capabilities means the variation of needs can be respected. This makes it possible to ask why children need more protein than adults or, more generally, why some need more care than others and why that care must be individualized.[15] Nussbaum thinks, moreover, that such care is rightly understood to be a matter of justice.

One cannot help but be sympathetic with Nussbaum's attempt to acknowledge the needs of the disabled. But it is not clear that the concept of capabilities advances justice. The very notion of capabilities depends on close analysis of practices that allow us to correlate the needs of a particular person with what will satisfy those needs. But that kind of concreteness is not available as long as Nussbaum is determined to maintain Rawls's liberal framework.[16] It's the same problem all over again: when we try to imagine politics without the contingencies of human life, people with disabilities get in the way.

Alan Ryan rightly observes that it is not as if Nussbaum is not persuasive about the needs and capacities of the disabled. The problem, he thinks, is that it is not clear why our—and by "our" I assume he means those of us who are not disabled—relation to the disabled is a matter of injustice. What, Ryan asks,

> would be lost by saying that the duties are stringent, inescapable, and urgent, but not duties of justice? Nussbaum shows—over and over—that no theory that explains justice as a contract for mutual advantage will show that these duties toward the disabled are a matter of justice. There may be little mutual advantage for the person who helps Arthur. Do we need a different theory of justice or should we say that many duties are grounded directly in the needs of beings to whom duties are owed, but are not a matter of justice? What difference does it make which we say?[17]

Nussbaum might well say in response that it makes all the difference what we say because if we do not understand what is done in the care of Sesha, Arthur and Jamie, we may abandon them to a world that cannot be trusted to care for them. They are lucky because they had parents that cared, but what happens if you do not have parents that care? The problem with Nussbaum's attempt to provide a theory to insure that Sesha, Arthur and Jamie be cared for is that it is just that—a theory. It is a theory, moreover, in which the wound of loneliness is a necessity so that we might be protected from one another and the disabled.

In contrast, Reinders argues that there is no point in arguing with a skeptical spectator that he or she should care about the disabled. Instead, he says, it is crucial for a liberal society that people exist who are willing to engage in the practice of caring for the disabled. According to Reinders, no public policy or theory can resolve the problem of what appears to be the burden of the lives of the disabled unless "it can tap resources that motivate citizens to value the commitment that it requires."[18] After all, significance found in sharing one's life with another person—a significance that will usually come as a surprise—cannot be found outside the activity itself.

This admittedly lengthy consideration of political theory finally brings me back to the gentleness that characterizes the work of L'Arche. In an early essay, "L'Arche: Its History and Vision," Jean provides an account of how he became Jean Vanier. He notes that he first met people with mental disabilities in 1963. Father Thomas Philippe, a Dominican priest, was a chaplain for a home of thirty men in a small village called Trosly-Breuil. Jean was teaching philosophy at St. Michael's College at the University of Toronto, but through Father Thomas he met and began to live with Philippe and Raphael in Trosly. Jean reports,

> We began living together, buying food, cooking, cleaning, working in the garden, etc. I knew really nothing about the needs of handicapped people. All I wanted to

do was to create community with them. Of course, I did have a tendency to tell them what to do; I organized and planned the day without asking their opinion or desire. I suppose this was necessary in some ways, for we did not know each other and they came from a very structured situation. But I had a lot to learn about listening to the needs of handicapped people; I had a lot to discover about their capacity to grow.[19]

This is where political theory hits the ground. Nussbaum wants to give Jean justifications for helping the disabled. What she can't do is give him a reason to live with them. But that's exactly what Jean says he needed. He had to be taught how to be gentle. It is not easy to learn to be gentle with the mentally disabled. As Jean has already said, they also suffer from the wound of loneliness. They can ask for too much. Which means gentleness requires the slow and patient work necessary to create trust. Crucial for the development of trust is that assistants in L'Arche discover the darkness, brokenness and selfishness shaped by their own loneliness. Remember, all assistants come to L'Arche already shaped by the political assumptions I've described. According to Jean, through the struggle to discover that we are wounded like the mentally disabled, we discover how much "we need Jesus and his Paraclete. For without them we cannot enter into this life of compassion and communion with our weaker brothers and sisters."[20]

In case anyone wonders if Jean recognizes the political implications of what he has learned, he tells us that through his contact with men and women with intellectual disabilities,

> I discovered then how divided and fragmented our societies are. On the one hand are those who are healthy and well integrated into society; on the other are those who are excluded, on its margins. As in Aristotle's day, there are still masters and slaves. I realized that peace could not prevail while no attempt was made to span the gulf separating different cultures, different religions, and even different individuals.[21]

Jean Vanier wrote his dissertation on Aristotle. He knows well that Aristotle thought the test of any good polity was its ability to sustain friendship between people of virtue. Aristotle distinguishes three types of friendship. A "friendship of use" lasts only as long as you need the other person. This is what we now call a "business relationship." A "friendship of pleasure" lasts as long as people enjoy one another. "Friendship of virtue," however, depends on people who are equals seeing virtue in one another. But Aristotle would not have thought it possible for a friendship to exist between people who are mentally disabled and those who are not. Jean believes that friendship is what L'Arche is about. This is not only a challenge to Aristotle's understanding of friendship, it also calls into question the presupposition of liberal political theory that tries to envision a politics in which friendship is an afterthought.

That is why I am bold to suggest that the gentle character of the practices constituting the work of L'Arche are not peculiar to L'Arche, but rather necessary for any polity that would be about the goods held in common. For gentleness requires, as Reinders observes, that we learn to see that

> the other person is "given" to us in the sense that, prior to rules and principles of social morality, the presence of the other in our lives constitutes our responsibility. Moral responsibility arises neither from contractual relationships nor from the cooperative exchange between independent individuals. Instead it arises from the nature of the moral self that discovers itself within a network of social relationships. . . . The benefits bestowed by love and friendship are consequential rather than conditional, which explains why human life that is constituted by these relationships is appropriately experienced as a gift. A society that accepts responsibility for dependent others such as the mentally disabled will do so because there are sufficient people who accept something like this account as true.[22]

Long story short: we don't get to make our lives up. We get to receive our lives as gifts. The story that says we should have no story except the story we chose when we had no story is a lie. To be human is to learn that we don't get to make up our lives because we're creatures. Christians are people who recognize that we have a Father whom we can thank for our existence. Christian discipleship is about learning to receive our lives as gifts without regret. And that has the deepest political implications. Much of modern political theory and practice is about creating a society where we do not have to acknowledge that our lives are gifts we receive from one another.

These are not small matters. In their book *Cultural Locations of Disability*, Sharon Snyder and David Mitchell advocate a cultural model of disability that makes possible "a political act of renaming that designates disability as a site of resistance and a source of cultural agency previously suppressed—at least to the extent that groups can successfully rewrite their own definition in view of a damaging material and linguistic heritage."[23] In other words, they want to see the disabled resist the labels of society by claiming power. Such resistance is necessary, they argue, because the very designation of disability in modernity represented a scourge and a promise: "Its very presence signaled a debauched present of cultural degeneration that was tending to regress toward a prior state of primitivism, while at the same time it seemed to promise that its absence would mark the completion of modernity as a cultural project."[24] But I confess I am not convinced that a cultural studies model of disability will provide the resistance they so desire. Ultimately, I suspect it draws on the same ethos that Nussbaum assumes.

Instead, I think Jean has already given us the kind of gift we need to help us overwhelm the wound of loneliness that grips our lives in the name of freedom. Jean rightly thinks of the gift of L'Arche as political. Without examples like L'Arche, we will assume there is no alternative to the politics of distrust that comes from the wound of our loneliness. I fear that many of us, like Daniel, feel guilty for existing and, as a result, seek to protect ourselves with thick walls so we will not have to acknowledge our vulnerability. Jean exemplifies a way for us to be with one another that we could have never "thought up." I had a pastor for many years who would often look out at us in the congregation and say, "That you're here is a miracle. I couldn't have thought up or imagined the church. God did." We couldn't have thought up or imagined L'Arche. God did. We do well, therefore, to attend to the lessons of L'Arche on how to be, even in the most difficult relationships, gentle. If we will listen, we can learn from Jean's story how to receive the givenness of life without regret.

God and Gentleness

To try to suggest the political significance of gentleness seems quite enough a task for a small book like this. But I cannot conclude without exploring what may be an even greater challenge. Put simply, I wonder if the kind of gentleness we see in L'Arche is possible without God. Jean's written work is suffused with his unmistakable

Catholic convictions and piety. Indeed, in many of the quotations from his work that I have already cited, he makes clear that without Jesus and the Holy Spirit the work of L'Arche would be impossible.

Yet in *Made for Happiness* Jean observes that though many people today have no religious faith, it remains important for us to communicate with them at a rational level in order to reflect on things human. He rightly says that many of Aristotle's insights are valid for any ethics. As Jean sees it, being human does not consist in obeying laws. Rather, to be human "means becoming as perfectly accomplished as possible. If we do not become fully accomplished, something is lost to the whole of humanity. For Aristotle this accomplishment derives from the exercise of the most perfect activity: that of seeking the truth in all things, shunning lies and illusions, acting in accordance with justice, transcending oneself to act for the good of others in society."[25]

I have no reason to question Jean's use of Aristotle as a way to sustain a conversation with those who do not share his Christian convictions. With Charles Pinches I have explored some of the same resources that Aristotle provides for helping Christians understand what it means to be Christian.[26] With Jean I believe we were created for happiness, which turns out, as Aquinas suggests, to be nothing less than friendship with God. Frankly, I can't imagine anything more frightening than that. Just think, for example, how frightening it is to be befriended by other people in community and have to hear their stories. How could we ever become friends of God? Surely friendship with God requires a transformation of self not unlike learning to be gentle by becoming friends with a person as unlike me as the mentally disabled. Accordingly, Aristotle can help us make connections with those who do not share our faith, but it remains the case that what we believe as Christians may finally "explode" Aristotle's categories, just as Thomas Aquinas demonstrated in his great work.

Which means, I think, that if gentleness is a virtue constitutive of politics, then Christians cannot help but be in tension with the liberal political arrangements in which we find ourselves. One of the reasons Nussbaum finds a Rawlsian account attractive in spite of its exclusion of the disabled is that such an account

> is articulated in terms of freestanding ethical ideas only, without reliance on metaphysical and epistemological doctrines (such as those of the soul, or revelation, or the denial of either of these) that would divide citizens along lines of religion or comprehensive ethical doctrine. It is therefore hoped that this conception can be the object of an overlapping consensus among citizens who otherwise have different comprehensive views.[27]

So politics as we know it is arranged to make strong religious convictions secondary by making them private. If gentleness is indeed both rooted in our relationship with God and somehow intrinsic to political arrangements, we begin to see why the politics of L'Arche might put us in tension with our present social arrangements. Which makes it all the more important that L'Arche not hide its lamp under a bushel basket. If L'Arche loses its theological voice, I think it will be a loss not only for L'Arche but for any politics, and in particular those determined by liberal political arrangements, in which L'Arche exists.

All I am asking is for Jean to be willing to wash the feet of those who do not share his faith. In his commentary on the Gospel of John, Jean reflects on the problem of power by commenting on Jesus' washing of his disciples' feet (John 13:1-17). He notes that all societies are built on the model of a pyramid with the powerful, the rich and the intelligent at the top. Yet Jesus takes the place of the slave by washing his disciples' feet. Jean confesses that he is deeply moved when someone with disabilities washes his feet. That someone with disabilities should wash his feet is why the politics of the gospel is, as Jean puts it, of a "world upside down."[28]

Jean observes that it is tempting for those that would wash the feet of the disabled to assume the model of the pyramid of power in the name of the service they perform. For example, he suggests that after the conversion of Constantine in 313, church and state became intertwined with the result that many bishops and abbots acted as if they were princes and lords. The dominant habits of the society became the habits of the church, thus corrupting the church. Yet Francis of Assisi came refusing to attack the institution of the church, which included many good people, but chose the other way by his commitment to the poor.[29]

Reflecting on Francis's admonitions to the heads of his fraternities, Jean notes,

> Followers of Jesus will continually be caught up in the paradox. Shepherds, teachers and leaders are necessary. They have power, but how should they exercise that power in the spirit of the gospels? How should they give a clear message about the truth of Jesus' message? How should they speak out against the powers of wealth? How should they be servant-leaders who humbly give their lives?[30]

Jean answers: "When the poor and weak are present, they prevent us from falling into the trap of power—even the power to do good—of thinking that it is we who are the good ones, who must save the Savior and his church."[31] I take this to mean that the politics of gentleness cannot be a triumphalistic politics. So it is all the more important that the theological voice of L'Arche not be silenced in the name of trying to reconcile people who come from diverse backgrounds and religious traditions. It is not for us as Christians to regret the loss of Christendom. But the loss of Christian structures and institutions makes it all the more important that the gentle care exemplified by Jesus in washing his disciples' feet—that gentleness exemplified in L'Arche—be unapologetically a witness to the One who would save us through the cross. Otherwise how would the world know that our loneliness has been overwhelmed and it is possible for us to trust one another?

Conclusion

L'Arche as a Peace Movement

JOHN SWINTON

*The fundamental principle of peace is a belief
that each person is important.*

Jean Vanier

*I believe one of the singular gifts L'Arche has made
for Christian and non-Christian alike is to help
us see what peace looks like.*

Stanley Hauerwas

*O*therwise how would the world know that our loneliness has been overwhelmed and it is possible for us to trust one another?"

What a wonderful question. A world that is immersed in violence and meaninglessness and that has lost sight of the story that makes sense of all other stories needs to know that trust is possible. Such a world needs to know that despite the violence of the world, peace remains not only possible but observable. The cross of Christ may well have overcome the darkness of the world, but sometimes we just need to see that. We long to see peace while we are longing for it.

In a recent essay Stanley Hauerwas describes L'Arche as a peace movement.[1] He observes that in recent years Jean Vanier has begun to emphasize that the L'Arche communities are places that exemplify peace. Indeed, Hauerwas suggests, Vanier is rapidly coming to the position where he sees the exemplification of peace as an essential task of L'Arche. In line with the issues raised in this book, Vanier continues to draw our attention to fear as a source of violence. Perfect love overcomes fear, but fear turns us in on ourselves and opens us to the possibility of violence. As Hauerwas puts it:

The fear that dominates our lives is not in the first

instance the fear of an enemy, unless it is acknowledged that each of us is the enemy, but rather the fear that is the source of violence is the fear that makes us unwilling to acknowledge the wounded character of our lives. L'Arche is a place where the wounds of each person cannot avoid being exposed and thus hopefully healed, becomes a context where we can learn the patient habits necessary for peace. Vanier knows such an understanding of peace may not have results for creating a more peaceful world at the international level, but he suggests "we are all called to become men and women of peace wherever we may be—in our family, at work, in our parish, in our neighborhood."[2]

This is precisely what the essays in this book offer us: ways of becoming people of peace wherever we may be. They invite us to recognize that history and time do not belong to us but are gifts from God that have purpose and direction. We have no option other than to live in a world that was created by God and that God promises to guide through to its rightful conclusion. We may at times wish that not to be the case! We may wish that we could escape from Providence and live peaceably within our own time. But the violence of this world indicates that such a wish and the desire to reside within "our own time" only serves to create an illusory space within which we encounter the pain of the world without hope or the possibility of transformation and reconciliation with God. None of us would wish to dwell in that space for long. We live in God's time and within God's history. The salvation of the world is God's task, not ours. Our task is to be faithful, peaceful people wherever we are. And the shape of that peace is determined not by the violence of the world, but rather by the recognition that Jesus who is gentle has redeemed time and that the key to faithful living is living trustfully, patiently and gently until the Lord returns (James 5:7).

L'Arche reminds us that time is not simply a commodity to be wasted, spent, saved or used but is rather a gift given to us so that we might pursue the things of the kingdom. The people living in L'Arche have recognized that time is a gift.[3] When we are freed from the tyranny of time, we can begin to look differently at the world, and when we look differently we begin to recognize just what an odd place it is. When we look at the world in this way we are no longer bound by the dangerous illusion that our "ultimate destiny and happiness is tied to how we 'spend' [our] time." Thus we discover the reality of a "new time"; "a time for caring for those who do not promise to make the world a better place, a time for being with those who do not promise to contribute to our status, a time for entering into the gratuitous and joyful worship of a God who does not promise that things will always work out 'right.' A time to wait patiently until the Lord returns."[4]

L'Arche lays down a marker in the fabric of time, a marker

reminding us that in Jesus, time has been redeemed for the practices of peace. Its presence reminds us that Christianity is not a theory but a practice. To believe in Christianity we need not only to know about God; we need to see God, to feel God and to love God in all things and at all times. That is our peace, our shalom. Peace follows the shape of the gospel; it needs to be seen to be believed. L'Arche helps us to begin to see what peace looks like.

Blessed are the peacemakers, for they will be called sons of God.

Jesus

Study Guide

INTRODUCTION: LIVING GENTLY IN A VIOLENT WORLD

1. What motivated you to read this book? What do you hope to gain by reading it?

2. What is your experience with disability? Have you, a family member or a friend been labeled "disabled"? Have you been labeled "normal"? How has that labeling affected your life?

3. John Swinton explains that this book is about learning to see the world differently by listening to the voices of those who already see differently due to their life experiences. What did you learn by listening to the story of Angela (pp. 12-13)? What did you learn from Dianne (pp. 13-15)?

4. How are the truths of the so-called normal world actually quite odd? What does it say about the assumptions of "normal" people that we "develop policies and practices that welcome people with disabilities into our communities, offering them rights and responsibilities, and at precisely the same time we develop forms of

genetic technology designed to prevent them from entering society at all"?

5. Why do we misunderstand the abortion of babies with Down syndrome as an act of compassion? How is this a misunderstanding?

6. L'Arche is a community in which people with and without disabilities live together. Swinton explains that L'Arche is about "living with" rather than "doing for." What is at stake in this distinction? How does it change the nature of a relationship?

7. After reading the introduction, what challenges do you think you might face in hearing and receiving this book? What will be difficult? What has already come as good news?

Chapter 1: The Fragility of L'Arche and the Friendship of God

1. What do you think of when you hear the phrase "disabled person"? Do you typically think of learning lessons from the disabled? If so, what sorts of lessons?

2. Vanier describes L'Arche on page 25 as a "fragile reality." What are the ways that it is fragile? What obstacles has L'Arche had to overcome? What can we learn from the fragility of L'Arche?

3. Vanier describes transformation as the disappearance of "the walls separating us from others and from our deepest self . . . walls built on loneliness and the absence of God, walls built on fear" (p. 26). What are the walls in your life? What can we learn about transformation from the stories of Janine and the seventeen-year-old assistant?

4. Describe the "gap" between the "so-called 'normal' world and the people who have been pushed aside, put into institutions, excluded from our societies because they are weak and vulnerable or even killed before birth" (p. 29). How does L'Arche respond to this gap? How might you respond to this gap?

5. How does Vanier explain God's preference for the weak as described in 1 Corinthians 1? What can we learn about living with God from those who are crying out for love?

6. What does Vanier mean by the "holiness" of the poor and disabled?

7. Re-read Luke 14:12-14. What can we learn from Jesus' instructions in this text? How might you implement this sort of eating and living in your life or church?

8. How does your church follow the injunction from 1 Corinthians 12 that "the weakest and least presentable are most necessary to the body and should be

honored" (p. 36)? How could you or your church follow 1 Corinthians 12 more closely?

9. Vanier explains that at L'Arche, to celebrate means to affirm that "you are a gift. You're a gift to the community" (p. 38). What is so radical about this idea of celebration? How is this different than other ways of celebrating? What would it look like for you to celebrate in this way?

10. What are some of the lessons from throughout this chapter that Vanier suggests we learn from the disabled? How could you enact those lessons in your life?

CHAPTER 2: FINDING GOD IN STRANGE PLACES

1. Do you like to move slowly? When have you found it important to slow down? When do you find it frustrating?

2. Hauerwas suggests that L'Arche teaches the church to slow down. Why is this so important? What are some of the negative effects of a culture of speed? How does L'Arche embody a different way of patience?

3. How does L'Arche teach the significance of place and "constancy of place"? How do routine and constancy not become boring?

4. On page 49, Hauerwas tells the story of the thirty-six-inch snowstorm. What can we learn from that story about technology and community?

5. Hauerwas writes, "L'Arche stands as a reminder that 'progress' should not mean eliminating all that threatens us" (p. 52). How does L'Arche teach that lesson? What does that mean for medical ethics? What does that mean in your political life? What might that mean in your personal life?

6. What would it look like for "Christians to learn to be hope in a world where there is no solution" (p. 55)? What does that mean? How does L'Arche embody hope without solution?

7. What is the difference between "curing" and "caring"? How does L'Arche reveal the limits of "curing" and call for increased "caring"?

8. On page 57, Stanley compares L'Arche to early monasticism. What reforms might L'Arche be suggesting for the church? How are these difficult or challenging?

9. How do you understand disability differently after reading this chapter? How do you understand your own life and assumptions differently? How might God be calling you to change?

CHAPTER 3: THE VISION OF JESUS

1. What are some of the hardest walls to break down in your city? In your personal life?

2. How does fear create walls between people? What do you fear? What do you do to protect yourself from what you fear? How does that create walls in your life?

3. Vanier talks about the "mystery" of people with disabilities on pages 65-66. What does he mean by that? What mysteries do you see in the lives of Francoise or the businessman and his wife who has Alzheimer's? Where is God in these stories?

4. Describing what he has learned by welcoming people with disabilities, Vanier writes, "When we welcome the broken outside, they call us to discover the broken inside" (p. 67). How have you learned of your own brokenness and weakness by welcoming others?

5. How does L'Arche offer a prophetic witness in a culture that encourages the abortion of babies with disabilities? How does that culture of abortion affect the self-image of people currently living with disabilities? How does it affect the self-image of "normal" people?

6. Dr. Martin Luther King Jr. and Vanier describe the human need to have someone below us to show we are better off. How do you see this need in your city and in the world? How do you see it in yourself?

7. Vanier affirms again and again throughout this chapter that Jesus loves us just the way we are. Why is this difficult for us to accept? Who are we tempted to think Jesus does not love as they are?

8. On page 74, Vanier explains that the weakest and least presentable being indispensable to the body of Christ is "the heart of faith, of what it means to be the church." How would your church look different if you believed this? How would your life look different?

CHAPTER 4: THE POLITICS OF GENTLENESS

1. Who would you call gentle? What characterizes that person's life?

2. What does Hauerwas mean by "gentleness"? What stories and images stand out from this chapter that show what it means to be gentle?

3. On pages 79-80, Vanier explains that while relationships with the disabled might start with an impulse of generosity, they must move to a posture of listening. What is at stake in moving from generosity to listening? How would our church ministries look different if they were defined by listening instead of generosity?

4. Hauerwas suggests with Hans Reinders that our political life is based on the assumption that "individuals are

free to live their own lives as they prefer, provided that they allow other people freedom to do the same, and provided that they accept and receive a fair share of the burden and benefits of social cooperation" (pp. 81-82). Why is this assumption unable to make sense of disabled people? When do these assumptions break down for "normal" people?

5. Why is it problematic to define personhood according to the capacity for reason and free will? Who is excluded from being a person according to those values? What sorts of things does Jesus value in people?

6. How do Vanier and Hauerwas describe the political implications of what they have learned at L'Arche (see in particular pp. 89-91)?

7. Why does Stanley distinguish between "mak[ing] our lives up" and "receiv[ing] our lives as gifts" (p. 93)? What do these two models look like when lived out? What is our posture toward other people in each model? How does the Christian story fit or not fit with each model?

8. How is L'Arche a sign of an alternative to a "politics of distrust"? What might this alternative politics look like?

9. How might becoming friends with a disabled person teach you to become friends with God?

10. What do Vanier and Hauerwas learn from the foot-washing story in John 13? How can we apply this story to our social and political life? How might you live out this story in your life?

Conclusion: L'Arche as a Peace Movement

1. What do you think peace looks like?

2. Vanier writes, "The fundamental principle of peace is a belief that each person is important." How can you see this to be true, either from the stories in this book or from your own life? Who do you need to work on valuing? How might peace emerge from treating that person or group as important?

3. L'Arche has taught Hauerwas that the fear that creates violence is not first a fear of an enemy but the fear of our own wounds and weakness. How are you wounded and weak? How do you try to hide that from others? How might your relationships with others open up if you faced and shared those wounds?

4. What ideas has this book given you about how to become a "person of peace" right where you are?

5. How does feeling like you have a scarcity of time affect your life? How does it cause you to overlook the needs of other people or even your own needs? What

does L'Arche teach us about time and patience? How can those lessons lead us to peace?

6. How will you move forward after reading this book? How have you been changed? How will you relate differently toward others and the world?

7. How could your local congregation learn from the witness of L'Arche? What concrete proposals might you bring to your congregation after reading this book?

Notes

Introduction

[1] It was interesting to hear my friend and colleague Graham Monteith make a plea at the conference in Aberdeen, from which these essays emerged, for people with physical disabilities to be reconciled and redeemed from stigmatizing attitudes that often separate them from people with intellectual disabilities. Even within the disability community there is a hierarchy within which people with intellectual disabilities often find themselves at the bottom.

[2] In John Swinton, *Raging with Compassion: Pastoral Responses to the Problem of Evil* (Grand Rapids: Eerdmans, 2007), p. 191.

[3] See John Swinton and Elaine Powrie, *Why Are We Here?: Meeting the Spiritual Needs of People with Learning Disabilities* (London: Mental Health Foundation, 2004); and John Swinton, *A Space to Listen: Meeting the Spiritual Needs of People with Learning Disabilities* (London: Mental Health Foundation, 2002).

[4] Swinton and Powrie, *Why Are We Here?* p. 16.

[5] See T. S. Kuhn, *The Structure of Scientific Revolutions* (Chicago: University of Chicago Press, 1996).

[6] Stanley Hauerwas, *Within the Grain of the Universe: The Church's Witness and Natural Theology* (London: SCM Press, 2001), p. 214.

[7] Stanley Hauerwas, "Seeing Peace: L'Arche as a Peace Movement" (paper presented at the Templeton Foundation conference in Trosly, France, 2007).

[8] Stanley Hauerwas, *The Hauerwas Reader*, ed. John Berkman and Michael Cartwright (Durham, N.C.: Duke University Press, 2001), p. 100.

[9]For more on the history of Vanier and L'Arche, see Kathryn Spink, *The Miracle, the Message, the Story: Jean Vanier and L'Arche* (Mahwah, N.J.: Hidden-Spring, 2006).

[10]For a deeper exegesis of the importance of timefulness, see Stanley Hauerwas, "Timeful Friends," in *Critical Reflections on Stanley Hauerwas' Theology of Disability*, ed. John Swinton (Binghamton, N.Y.: Haworth, 2004) with a response by Jean Vanier.

[11]In Gilbert Milaender, "Learning from Pieper: On Being Lutheran in This Time and Place," *Concordia Theological Quarterly* 63, no. 1 (1999): 37-49.

Chapter 1: The Fragility of L'Arche and the Friendship of God

[1]John Paul II, "Message of John Paul II on the Occasion of the International Symposium on the Dignity and Rights of the Mentally Disabled Person" (January 2004), Vatican <www.vatican.va/holy_father/john_paul_ii/speeches/2004/january/documents/hf_jp-ii_spe_20040108_handicapmentale_en.html>.

[2]Etty Hillesum, *An Interrupted Life* (New York: Henry Holt, 1996), p. 178.

Chapter 2: Finding God in Strange Places

[1]The article is in Stanley Hauerwas, *Christian Existence Today: Essays on Church, World, and Living In Between* (Durham, N.C.: Labyrinth, 1988), pp. 253-66. The book, beginning in 2001, is published by Brazos.

[2]Patience is at the heart of John Howard Yoder's understanding of peace. See his "'Patience' as a Method in Moral Reasoning: Is an Ethic of Discipleship 'Absolute'?" in *The Wisdom of the Cross: Essays in Honor of John Howard Yoder*, ed. Stanley Hauerwas, Chris Huebner, Harry Huebner and Mark Thiessen Nation (Grand Rapids: Eerdmans, 1999), pp. 24-42.

[3]Paul Virilio, *Popular Defense and Ecological Struggles* (New York: Semiotext(e), 1990), p. 92; and *Identity* (Scottsdale, Penn.: Herald, 2006), pp. 119-20.

Chapter 3: The Vision of Jesus

[1]Patrick Viveret, *Reconsiderez la Richesse* (Paris: L'Aube, 2003).

Chapter 4: The Politics of Gentleness

[1]Jean Vanier, *Community and Growth* (London: Darton, Longman and Todd, 1979), p. 220.

[2]Ibid., pp. 25-26.

[3]Ibid., pp. 97-98.

[4]Ibid., p. 94.

[5]Jean Vanier, *Drawn into the Mystery of Jesus Through the Gospel of John* (New York: Paulist, 2004), p. 145.

[6]Hans Reinders, *The Future of the Disabled in Liberal Society: An Ethical Analysis* (Notre Dame, Ind.: University of Notre Dame Press, 2000), p. 14.

[7]Ibid., pp. 15-16.

[8]Martha Nussbaum, *Frontiers of Justice: Disability, Nationality, Species Membership* (Cambridge, Mass.: Harvard University Press, 2006), p. 17.

[9]Ibid., pp. 96-98.

[10]Ibid., p. 53.

[11]Ibid., p. 16.

[12]Ibid., p. 18.

[13]Ibid., pp. 113-14.

[14]Ibid., p. 160.

[15]Ibid., p. 170.

[16]Alan Ryan, "Cosmopolitans," *New York Review of Books* LIII (June 22, 2006), pp. 48-49.

[17]Ibid., p. 49.

[18]Reinders, *Future of the Disabled*, p. 207.

[19]Jean Vanier, "L'Arche: Its History and Vision," in *The Church and Disabled Persons*, ed. Griff Hogan (Springfield, Ill.: Templegate, 1983), p. 52.

[20]Ibid., p. 59.

[21]Jean Vanier, *Made for Happiness: Discovering the Meaning of Life with Aristotle*, trans. Kathryn Spink (London: DLT, 2001), p. xiii.

[22]Reinders, *Future of the Disabled*, p. 17.

[23]Sharon Snyder and David Mitchell, *Cultural Locations of Disability* (Chicago: University of Chicago Press, 2006), p. 10.

[24]Ibid., p. 31.

[25]Vanier, *Made for Happiness*, p. xiv.

[26]Stanley Hauerwas and Charles Pinches, *Christians Among the Virtues: Theological Conversations with Ancient and Modern Ethics* (Notre Dame, Ind.: University of Notre Dame Press, 1997), pp. 3-51.

[27]Nussbaum, *Frontiers of Justice*, p. 163.

[28]Vanier, *Drawn into the Mystery*, p. 228.

[29]Ibid., pp. 236-37.

[30]Ibid., pp. 237-38.

[31]Ibid., p. 238.

Conclusion

[1]Stanley Hauerwas, "Seeing Peace: L'Arche as a Peace Movement" (paper presented at the Templeton Foundation conference in Paris, France, 2007).

[2]Jean Vanier quoted by Kathryn Spink in *The Miracle, the Message, the Story: Jean Vanier and L'Arche* (Mahwah, N.J.: HiddenSpring, 2006).

[3]In my reflections on time in this section I am indebted to Philip Kenneson's analysis of Stanley Hauerwas's thinking (Philip Kenneson, "Taking Time for the Trivial: Reflection on Yet Another Book from Hauerwas," *The Asbury Theological Journal* 45, no. 1 [1990]).

[4]Kenneson, "Taking Time," p. 72.

About the Authors

Stanley Hauerwas (Ph.D., Yale University) is Gilbert T. Rowe Professor Emeritus of Divinity and Law at Duke Divinity School, Duke University. He was named "America's Best Theologian" by *Time* magazine and has written on the theological significance of disability. One of the most widely read theologians of the late twentieth century, his books include *Resident Aliens, Wilderness Wanderings, A Community of Character, A Peaceable Kingdom, Sanctify Them in the Truth, With the Grain of the Universe* and *A Better Hope.*

Jean Vanier (Ph.D., L'Institut Catholique de Paris) is the founder of L'Arche, an international network of communities where people with and without intellectual disabilities experience life together as fellow human beings who share a mutuality of care and need. Today over 147 L'Arche communities exist in 35 countries on five continents. Vanier is also the founder with Marie Hélène Mathieu of Faith and Light, communities of welcome and friendship that bring together people with intellectual disabilities, their parents and friends. There are now 1500 Faith and Light communities in 82 countries. Vanier's books include *Life's Great Questions, Community and Growth,*

Becoming Human, From Brokenness to Community and *Befriending the Stranger.* Vanier won the Templeton Prize in 2015.

John Swinton (Ph.D., Aberdeen) is chair in divinity and religious studies in the School of Divinity, History and Philosophy at the University of Aberdeen, and founder of the Centre for Spirituality, Health and Disability, which sponsored the conference that brought Hauerwas and Vanier together for this conversation. His books include *Raging with Compassion: Pastoral Responses to the Problem of Evil* and *Theology, Disability and the New Genetics.*

For more information about L'Arche, visit:
www.larche.org
www.larcheusa.org

For more information about the Centre for Spirituality, Health and Disability, visit:
www.abdn.ac.uk/cshad